THE OBAMA EFFECT

THE OBAMA EFFECT

How the 2008 Campaign Changed
White Racial Attitudes

Seth K. Goldman and Diana C. Mutz

Russell Sage Foundation • New York

Library of Congress Cataloging-in-Publication Data

Goldman, Seth K.
 The Obama effect : how the 2008 campaign changed white racial attitudes / Seth K. Goldman and Diana C. Mutz.
  pages cm
 Includes bibliographical references and index.
 ISBN 978-0-87154-572-5 (pbk. : alk. paper) — ISBN 978-1-61044-824-6 (ebook)
 1. Presidents—United States—Election—2008. 2. United States—Race relations—Political aspects. 3. Whites—United States—Attitudes. 4. Post-racialism—United States. 5. Obama, Barack. I. Mutz, Diana Carole. II. Title.
 E906.G65 2014
 324.973'0932—dc23

2013041605

Text design by Suzanne Nichols.

RUSSELL SAGE FOUNDATION
112 East 64th Street, New York, New York 10065
10 9 8 7 6 5 4 3 2 1

To my parents,
Bruce and Beth Goldman, for always being there
SKG

To my parents, for their love and support
DCM

CONTENTS

LIST OF FIGURES & TABLES

ABOUT THE AUTHORS

Seth K. Goldman is Honors Assistant Professor of Communication at the University of Massachusetts, Amherst.

Diana C. Mutz is Samuel A. Stouffer Professor of Political Science and Communication at the University of Pennsylvania.

PREFACE

This book began, in a sense, long before the 2008 election when we undertook a review of research on the effects of mass media on stereotyping and prejudice for a chapter in an edited volume. The difficulty with doing such a review was that little research had actually been conducted on this central issue in social science—central, we say, because it is widely assumed that media portrayals of social out-groups are a primary cause of perceptions of these groups.

Our investigation led us back to the formative years of mass communication research in the 1940s, when scholars employed media "treatments" in efforts to reduce prejudice toward racial, ethnic, and religious minorities. But these efforts, blunt as they were, failed spectacularly. Only many years later, in the 1970s, did scholars again examine the impact of mass media on out-group attitudes, yet ironically these studies—and most of those since—have emphasized the negative impact of media on intergroup relations.

This recent emphasis strikes us as oddly one-sided: if media can produce prejudice, then logically it should also be able to reduce it. And that, quite appropriately, is the conclusion that our analyses of the 2008 presidential campaign and first term of the Obama administration led us to in this book. Although we had hoped only to have good news to report, we were forced to contend with the empirical reality that media exposure may reduce, as well as produce, prejudice depending on the volume and quality of out-group portrayals. Still, we hope our findings provide a corrective to the strict pessimism of recent decades by highlighting the benefits of media as a point of contact between members of different social groups.

Many people have contributed to the completion of this book. For critical feedback at various stages of this research, we thank Pat Egan, Richard Johnston, Susanna Dilliplane, Michael X. Delli Carpini, John Lapinski, Robert Hornik, Kim Gross, Paul Sniderman, Spencer Piston, and Jamie Druckman. Paul Allison deserves particular praise for fielding many statistical queries about fixed-effects panel models during the last several years. The two anonymous reviewers of this book offered several helpful suggestions, as did the anonymous reviewers of Seth's article-length study. Many participants at academic conferences also provided keen insights that aided in the development of this project. We also thank the staff at the Annenberg School for Communication at the University of Pennsylvania and the Department of Communication at the University of Massachusetts, Amherst.

This study was only possible because of the unusually rich array of data we had at our disposal. Most of our analyses rely on the 2008 National Annenberg Election Study, so we thank the Annenberg Public Policy Center and its director Kathleen Hall Jamieson for funding the panel survey. Richard Johnston served as co-principal investigator on the NAES project, helping to push the design in a direction that made these panel analyses possible. A grant from the Russell Sage Foundation (RSF) generously funded the additional wave of panel data that allowed us to assess change in white racial attitudes from the close of the 2008 campaign through fall 2010. Suzanne Nichols, the director of publications at RSF, has been wonderful to work with, providing just the right amount of pressure to push this project to completion. Cynthia Buck, our copyeditor at RSF, offered numerous improvements to the manuscript. Additional data on blacks' racial attitudes in 2010 came from the Institute for the Study of Citizens and Politics at the University of Pennsylvania (ISCAP). We would also like to acknowledge that parts of chapters 2 and 4 are based on prior publications in *The SAGE Handbook of Prejudice, Stereotyping, and Discrimination* (Mutz and Goldman 2010) and *Public Opinion Quarterly* (Goldman 2012).

Seth thanks the many friends, family, and colleagues who supported him during the last several years as he went from being a graduate student struggling to finish his dissertation to a post-doc trying to figure out what to do next to an assistant professor. Neither this book, nor the dissertation, nor much else really, would have been accomplished without the immense support and friendship of many people along the way. Seth first thanks his co-author, Diana Mutz, for serving as advisor, mentor, and cheerleader. What began as an academic pairing has grown into a true friendship, one that he looks forward to for years to come.

Additionally, Diana would like to thank Seth for having the foresight to pursue this project. It was his insistence on adding measures of racial attitudes in the beginning of the project—long before we knew Obama would be the Democratic nominee—that made this whole study possible. It is first and foremost Seth's ideas and efforts that brought this book to fruition.

For their friendship and support, Seth also thanks his Annenberg classmates and Philly friends Adrienne Shaw, Deb Wainwright, Katie Huber, Rebekah Nagler, Sarah Vaala, and Sarah Parvanta. Finally, to his family: Marc Wittlif and David Warner, his surrogate parents; Winna and John, his sister and brother-in-law; and Bruce and Beth Goldman, the most patient, loving, and supportive parents a kid could possibly ask for.

CHAPTER 1

The Impact of the Obama Campaign on White Racial Attitudes

Frederick Douglass, who escaped from slavery in 1838 to become a leading abolitionist, said that he had less than one chance in 60 million of becoming president.[1] One hundred and seventy years later, on November 4, 2008, Barack Hussein Obama became the first African American to win a presidential election. As one resident of New Orleans said, "I never dreamed in my lifetime that I would see a black man as President of the United States. I was a kid growing up under Jim Crow. We couldn't drink out of the same water faucet—but now it seems that America has changed."[2] Civil rights leader and U.S. representative John Lewis concurred: "This is unreal, it's unbelievable. But I tell you, the struggle, the suffering, the pain and everything that we tried to do to create a more perfect union, it was worth it."[3]

Obama's election in 2008 seemingly represented a breakthrough; he was the first African American to win a major party's presidential nomination, even before going on to win the presidency. As Harvard law professor Randall Kennedy put it, "Never before has a candidate so fully challenged the many inhibitions that have prevented people of all races, including African Americans, from seriously envisioning presidential power in the hands of someone other than a white American."[4] For white Americans, this book suggests, the effects of exposure to Obama during the campaign went well beyond a new capacity to envision a black man in the White House: white Americans' ongoing exposure to a heavily counterstereotypical black individual changed what came to mind when they thought about African Americans more generally. The event itself—Obama's campaign and subsequent election—changed white racial attitudes even as it was transpiring. The aim of this book is to look at how and why white racial attitudes changed during this period.

Despite the groundbreaking nature of Obama's election, a veritable cottage industry of academic research on this topic has focused almost exclusively on an old theme in the study of racial politics: the influence of white racial prejudice on vote choice. For example, the central conclusion in *Obama's Race: The 2008 Election and the Dream of a Post-Racial America* by Michael Tesler and David Sears is that the 2008 election was more polarized by racial attitudes than any other presidential election on record.[5] Likewise, the central point of Donald Kinder and Allison Dale-Riddle's *The End of Race?* is that racism was an important factor in the 2008 vote.[6]

Indeed, evidence consistently shows that prejudice cost Obama votes among white Americans. Combining various estimates from the studies just mentioned suggests that in a color-blind America Obama would have won about five percentage points more of the popular vote. This is politically consequential, to be sure, but is it really surprising that prejudice stopped some whites from voting for a black man? Would anyone have predicted otherwise?

After the election, many scholars suggested that it was indeed surprising that Obama's race influenced vote choice and cited a "conventional wisdom" that Obama transcended race—that his election signaled "the end of race" or a "postracial" America. If these terms are taken to mean that race is no longer a significant or important influence in American society, then such claims appear to be largely contrived and of dubious origin. We suggest that this thesis is one to which few, if any, ever actually subscribed at the time Obama was elected, and one that is far too easily blown away by the facts. As one observer, David Hollinger, commented, "What were those prophets of post-ethnicity and post-raciality smoking when they started talking in those terms? The gap between what is being refuted and what is being affirmed is a discursive Grand Canyon."[7] Precisely because this argument is so easy to refute, Hollinger suggests, it obscures other important questions.

Thus far, this "straw man" has garnered the bulk of attention in research regarding the Obama election. And the repeated decimation of this thesis has been taken to mean that there is little about the Obama campaign and election that is meaningful with respect to understanding race relations. Obviously, his campaign alone could not miraculously change the disadvantaged status of black Americans. Nor could it suddenly make all Americans color-blind. But in a "competition to show just how bad racism still is," as Hollinger describes it, scholars may have overlooked what may be a more surprising, and ultimately more practical, observation: during the course of the 2008 campaign, whites systematically declined in the extent to which they thought more highly of their own white in-group over African Americans.[8] This significant decline occurred during the brief period of only a few months when Barack Obama was campaigning to become president of the United States.

No one will be surprised to hear that our own study was not designed with this particular hypothesis in mind. Six months after this panel survey was launched in October 2007, it was still unclear whether Obama would even be the Democratic Party's nominee for president. Moreover, the dominant assumption among many social scientists has been that racial attitudes are highly stable, only changing slowly over the course of many years, if at all.[9] A growing body of research portrays intergroup conflict as a fundamental human characteristic that is passed down genetically, hardwiring people to separate the world into "us" and "them."[10] Nevertheless, over the course of only six months, white racial attitudes clearly changed in a systematic direction during the 2008 presidential campaign.

For some, Barack Obama's history-making nomination for president and ultimate victory on November 7, 2008, were powerful symbols of progress in American race relations. Yet the Obama campaign not only reflected change but was itself a contributing factor in reducing white racial prejudice. Our panel data allow us to show that the same individuals who were most exposed to the Obama campaign also exhibited the largest declines in racial prejudice.

This central finding was the impetus for our exploration of changes in racial attitudes. Our study draws on the 2008 National Annenberg Election Study's (NAES) large, nationally representative, five-wave panel survey to understand the beneficial effects of exposure to Obama during the campaign on racial prejudice. We started with an unusually large sample of 20,000 people and tried to interview them up to five times over the course of just over a year; thus, it was possible to analyze which people actually changed their views in a systematic direction during the course of a single campaign. Furthermore, our data allow us to link change in specific independent variables to individual change in racial attitudes.

Most research on the causes of racial attitudes has relied on cross-sectional samples rather than over-time panel evidence. As a result, we know a lot about the correlates of negative attitudes toward blacks, but relatively little about what changes racial attitudes over time. Experiments have done much better at helping us understand change, but this approach cannot be used to observe spontaneously occurring changes in racial attitudes as events naturally unfold.

In addition to panel analyses, this study was also designed to track gradual change in smaller aggregates from week to week. Continuous tracking was made possible by randomizing the date of each respondent's interview within each of the panel waves. In this fashion, each week's interviews could be treated as a separate random sample for purposes of tracking change during shorter periods of time within each wave. Although the week-to-week tracking of aggregates lacks the statistical power and explanatory capabilities of the individual-level panel data, it is extremely useful for confirming that the time of a particular data collection was not an abnormal, unrepresentative snapshot of what was actually transpiring over time. In short, we have benefited from a wealth of data on changes in racial attitudes during this period of time and have been able to martial this evidence toward an understanding of why the campaign affected white Americans as it did.

Figure 1.1 provides an overview of the trend that initially caught our attention. We plot levels of white racial prejudice from the summer of 2008 through Obama's inauguration in the winter of 2009. There is a gradual, but nonetheless clear, trend toward lower levels of white prejudice against blacks. Notably, this downward trend begins long before Obama is elected, and continues up to his inauguration.

In chapter 2, we discuss further the many difficulties of measuring prejudice. But here, consistent with many previous measures of racial prejudice, non-Hispanic whites were asked to rate both blacks and whites on a variety of different characteristics, including scales that tapped "hardworking" to "lazy," "intelligent" to "unintelligent," and "trustworthy" to "untrustworthy." At different points in the survey, and in a randomized order, whites were asked to rate their own racial group (their in-group) and blacks (their relative out-group). We calculated whites' level of "in-group favoritism," or racial prejudice, by looking at the difference between how positively individuals regarded their own racial group relative to African Americans. This is a standard and widely used measure of racial prejudice—one with demonstrable consequences for evaluations of race-related public policies and black political leaders.[11]

As seen in the past when this technique has been used to tap ethnocentrism more generally[12] or white-black prejudice more specifically,[13] overwhelmingly most people rate their own in-group more favorably than they do out-groups.

Figure 1.1   Aggregate Change in White Racial Prejudice During the 2008 Presidential Campaign

Source: 2008 NAES Panel Survey.

Note: Range is 0 to 100, where 0 indicates an absence of prejudice and higher positive values indicate higher levels of prejudice, although within each wave 95 percent or more of the values fall within a range of 0 to 40. Data are smoothed by fourteen-day prior moving average and are unweighted. For statistical tests of whether whites changed their racial attitudes significantly, we analyzed the data as a three-wave panel in a fixed-effects model of within-person change. The model predicts change in white racial prejudice based on time—that is, dummy variables for waves 4 and 5, with wave 3 as the excluded reference category—and controls for the order in which the racial groups (in-group and out-group) were asked about. The model shows significant within-person change from wave 3 to wave 4 (-1.07, $p < 0.001$) and from wave 3 to wave 5 (-2.08, $p < 0.001$) (N = 2,636). The means and standard deviations for waves 3, 4, and 5 are 8.16 (15.01), 7.10 (14.57), and 6.09 (13.20) (N = 2,636).

This was the case for whites' evaluations of themselves relative to blacks as well, so the average aggregate scores for all dates are positive. In other words, by our measure most white Americans exhibited racial prejudice before, during, and after the 2008 campaign. Nonetheless, a quick glance at figure 1.1 makes it clear that something happened, and it happened gradually over the course of a single campaign rather than over years or generations. The extent to which whites evaluated themselves more highly than African Americans changed in a consistently less prejudiced direction throughout the 2008 campaign.

The finding in figure 1.1 is the central puzzle motivating this book. Fortunately, we have an unusually rich compendium of data with which to explore this trend. First, we benefit from a large sample of panelists, each of whom provided three or more waves of panel data for most analyses. In addition, because the same people were surveyed multiple times during the course of the campaign, our analyses benefit from tremendous statistical power. Not only can we evaluate which kinds of people changed the most, but we also can assess change at the level of the individual in relation to change over time in potential causes. Although the overall trend is toward less prejudice, it inevitably masks the fact that some individuals became more negative toward blacks and others changed little, if at all. This individual-level variance is ultimately very useful in understanding what drives these changes over time.

In addition to measures of racial prejudice, our study also includes indicators of related concepts that aid us in understanding this trend, such as perceptions of race relations. Finally, and perhaps most importantly, our study includes unusually extensive means by which we can measure individual levels of exposure to the campaign itself so as to test a variety of competing theories that might explain this phenomenon.

We are not the first to suggest such an effect from the Obama campaign and election. In a recent article, Susan Welch and Lee Sigelman noted that white attitudes toward blacks were more positive in 2008 than in 2004, after little change during the preceding decade.[14] This observation prompted them to posit an "Obama Effect," whereby exposure to Obama's campaign reduced white racial prejudice. Because the data they had to work with were sparse—only one assessment every four years—and because there was some decline already visible since 1992, it was difficult for them to draw strong conclusions about whether this was a continuation of an earlier trend or an effect of Obama's emergence as an important figure in American politics. Moreover, the aggregate snapshots from every four years left open many plausible alternative interpretations. Nonetheless, Welch and Sigelman made a strong case that, at the very least, Obama's campaign accelerated the previous trend.[15]

Unfortunately, the current understanding of what moves racial attitudes is limited at best. Nonetheless, we think Welch and Sigelman's general idea is probably spot-on. The huge amount of media attention garnered by Obama during the campaign made him, at least for a period of time, by far the most prominent African American in the United States. As they suggest, "No other black elected official in the United States has been nearly as visible or salient as Obama has become."[16] During the campaign itself, Obama's image enjoyed greater prominence than that of any other African American—from any walk of life, political or otherwise. Although they could not pinpoint when these changes occurred or by what process, Welch and Sigelman concluded that between 2004 and 2008 whites' views of blacks became more positive, even more so than expected given the earlier trend.

Our study picks up where theirs left off. We posit a specific theoretical framework for understanding an "Obama Effect," drawing on social psychological research on the impact of prominent exemplars in changing attitudes toward out-groups. While some Americans liked Obama's politics and others did not, he was uniformly perceived to be an example of a highly successful, intelligent, and charismatic black American. As part of a highly accomplished and intact nuclear family, he directly contradicted many of the negative stereotypes held by white Americans about black men in particular. In experimental settings, exposure to counterstereotypical examples of African Americans has caused white subjects to express more positive views of blacks. For example, in one study, treatment subjects filled out a questionnaire that surreptitiously exposed them to likable and extremely successful African Americans such as Oprah Winfrey and Michael Jordan. In a later, seemingly unrelated questionnaire, these respondents who had been exposed to the counterstereotypical exemplars expressed less stereotypical views of African Americans. Either their stereotypes of blacks were improved through this exposure or their negative stereotypes were simply made less salient than more positive associations, thus leading to more positive overall evaluations.[17]

The flooding of white Americans' television screens with positive black exemplars is only one of several potential processes of influence that we explore. Most importantly, we suggest that instead of dismissing Obama's campaign as a "non-event" because it did not end racism, it is important for scholars to understand the change that did occur and how it was related to Obama's campaign and election. Particularly because ongoing racism is undoubtedly important, we need a better understanding of how and why racial attitudes change when they do. Experimental studies have given us some insight into this process, primarily into very short-term changes in laboratory settings, but predicting and documenting changes in racial attitudes as they occur naturally in the real world is no easy feat. In this case, because the trend was part of a well-documented, large-scale panel study surrounding the 2008 election, we have the opportunity to study a shift in racial attitudes more decisively than is usually possible. We also explore, using individual-level data, the probable causes of this change. Understanding the causes of change in racial attitudes provides the leverage needed to engineer still further change.

As a recent review of research on prejudice reduction noted, "It is ironic but not coincidental that the largest empirical literature on the subject of prejudice—namely, public opinion research on the subject of race and politics—has little, if any connection to the subject of prejudice reduction."[18] Despite the fact that public opinion research is central to our understanding of prejudice, as well as the source of most of our theories of prejudice, it treats prejudice as a stable attribute of individuals caused by long-term social forces beyond virtually anyone's control.

There are some notable exceptions to this generalization. For example, Zoltan Hajnal studied the effect of black mayors on white racial attitudes.[19] He suggests that the election of blacks to public office has consequential effects on whites' attitudes. These beneficial outcomes include reducing white fears about blacks and black leaders, improving race relations, and increasing the likelihood that they will subsequently vote for a black candidate. According to his theory, these changes occur because after a black mayor is elected, whites learn from this experience that their interests will not suffer under black leadership, and thus they become more positive in their attitudes toward blacks more generally: "The contrast between their fears and the reality is so stark," Hajnal notes, "that whites are forced to reevaluate blacks and black leadership."[20]

Of course, in the case of our evidence, it cannot have been the experience of having a black president serving in office that produced the benefits we documented. As we have seen, the beneficial effects occurred long before Obama had a chance to serve as president. Moreover, those benefits could not have derived from a lessening sense of economic competition between blacks and whites: this decline in negative out-group attitudes occurred at the same time that the economy was plunging into the Great Recession. By the time of the 2008 election, the severity of the economic decline was well known and could hardly be overlooked. This downward trend should have produced, if anything, increasing interracial tensions, according to realistic group conflict theory.[21] Given these issues, we turned to alternative theories that were a better fit to the timing and circumstances of this change.

As we describe at greater length in chapter 4, the theory that best explains this systematic trend is what we call mediated intergroup contact, operating by means of a process of exemplification.[22] In a nutshell, what this means is that during this period of time people were being exposed to unusually large amounts of media coverage of Obama, coverage that countered negative racial stereotypes. This mediated exposure served as a surrogate form of positive inter-group contact: when whites thought about African Americans, what came to mind was a highly salient positive exemplar, Barack Obama, as opposed to the many negative exemplars often seen on television.[23]

Although prejudice was certainly not eliminated during this short period of time leading up to the 2008 presidential election, many people—especially those with more negative initial views of African Americans—changed their attitudes in a more positive direction as a result of mediated exposure. Importantly, we think that these changes occurred largely without people's conscious awareness and independently of partisan politics as traditionally understood. In other words, it did not matter if people liked Obama-the-candidate or his policies. Instead, a far more subtle process of influence was at work. As Obama became increasingly prominent in the media, what came to people's minds when they thought of African Americans changed for the better.

Although mediated intergroup contact is certainly not the same as face-to-face contact, psychologists point out that it has many of the same advantages without some of the key drawbacks. In general, positive intergroup contact has been found to have beneficial effects for racial attitudes.[24] But one of the central impediments to the kind of contact that is beneficial is the anxiety that people experience in face-to-face interracial contexts. Anxiety and feelings of threat are known barriers to achieving the benefits of intergroup contact.[25] Moreover, those with high levels of anxiety are likely to avoid face-to-face intergroup encounters.[26]

In this respect, mediated intergroup contact is particularly advantageous because it provides opportunities for "contact" without the anxiety often char-acterizing face-to-face intergroup interactions. Other forms of "indirect" or "extended" contact have also been shown to improve out-group attitudes, such as learning that an in-group friend is friends with an out-group member.[27] Even imagining having face-to-face contact with an out-group member can improve attitudes toward the out-group as a whole, thus making the idea of mediated intergroup contact less far-fetched.[28]

If our theory is correct—if mediated exposure to Obama during the cam-paign did help to reduce racial prejudice—then we should expect to see a number of clear patterns in our results. First, the decline in white in-group favoritism should have occurred primarily because whites' attitudes toward blacks improved, not because whites' attitudes toward their own in-group became more critical. Second, the amount of change that occurred during the campaign should be large relative to what recent historical fluctuations suggest is typical for a six-month period. Third, if the process of influence operates irrespective of people's politics and partisanship, as exemplification theory suggests, then racial attitudes should improve even among Obama's political opponents. In fact, because conservatives, on average, typically have more negative views of blacks than liberals do, the Obama exemplar ought to contrast with their preexisting views the most, thus producing far more change than among those for whom a positive black exemplar is less unexpected. Fourth, and most importantly, whites who experienced the most exposure to Obama through the media should exhibit the largest improvements in their views of African Americans. We test these hypotheses in the chapters that follow.

THE ORGANIZATION OF THE BOOK

The remainder of the book carefully evaluates our central finding and several related patterns, while evaluating theoretical explanations as to why, under what conditions, and for what reasons positive change in racial attitudes appears to have occurred during the 2008 presidential campaign. In part I, we outline this puzzle in considerable depth: how is it that after decades of seeming stagnation in white racial attitudes in America, racial attitudes changed systematically and significantly during such a brief period of time? Chapter 2 explores the thorny issue of measuring racial attitudes in public opinion surveys. How can we be sure that the trends we observed are not an artifact of the way in which in-group and out-group attitudes were measured? Did people give more socially desirable answers in the context of increased attention to race? Looking for evidence of social desirability, assimilation, and contrast effects, we took advantage of the fact that fresh samples of respondents were added throughout the panel study, enabling us to examine possible panel conditioning effects and the impact of attrition on the representativeness of the sample. We were ultimately reassured that the change occurred, that it is worthy of our attention, and that it is sizable in historical perspective.

Part I also examines the extent to which other race-related attitudes changed during the 2008 campaign. Specifically, in chapter 3 we assess change over time in perceptions of race relations. Did whites also change their perceptions of how well whites and blacks are getting along with one another in American society? We examine trends in perceptions of past, present, and future race relations as the Obama campaign unfolded. Consistent with the trend in figure 1.1, chapter 3 shows that white perceptions of race relations became increasingly positive during the campaign, and that this was true whether people were asked retrospectively or prospectively about race relations. Thus, a sense of interracial optimism was clearly pervasive even before Obama's victory.

While documenting the changes that took place during this period of time, part I is largely descriptive in scope. In part II, we draw on a larger body of data to investigate a range of possible theoretical explanations for the trends described in part I. It is virtually certain that whatever it was about the campaign that influenced racial attitudes reached white Americans via mass media; whatever the impetus, only mass media could have brought something to mass public attention in this fashion. In chapter 4, we elaborate on the theory of mediated intergroup contact, arguing that extensive, mass mediated exposure to counterstereotypical images of Obama changed the kinds of associations that were most salient in whites' minds when they thought about African Americans. By using repeated measures of both exposure and racial attitudes, we explain change over time in white racial attitudes as a function of changes in the quality and quantity of media coverage. The innumerable images of Obama and his family, who sharply countered negative racial stereotypes, changed the balance of positive and negative black exemplars portrayed in mass media from mostly negative to mostly positive. Whereas the usual exemplars of blacks in mass media associate blacks with criminality, scandal, and poverty, Obama and his family looked like they were "out of central casting," as one broadcaster put it.[29] Consistent with this theory, whites who initially held the most negative stereotypes of blacks experienced the greatest improvement in racial prejudice during the campaign, and those who were likely to see Obama and his family as deviations from expectations were most affected.

Because we used a large-scale, multi-wave panel of whites for these analyses, we are able to make much stronger causal arguments than are allowed by most observational studies. Thus, we can establish that the changes were systematic rather than random fluctuations, and that they were tied to changes in media exposure. Nonetheless, mediated intergroup contact is not the only possible theoretical explanation. In chapter 5, we explore several plausible alternative interpretations by focusing greater attention on the specific kinds of media coverage about race that were prominent during this period. We use a large-scale analysis of media content to describe the major kinds of coverage that Obama's campaign received, focusing on key aspects of coverage that might change racial attitudes. Interestingly, we find that race and racism were at best minor themes during the campaign itself, and thus the capacity of the coverage of these themes to trigger widespread change in racial attitudes was limited. We rule out several rival theoretical explanations represented by other types of campaign coverage, such as discussion involving themes of racial unity between whites and blacks.

Finally, part III skips ahead from 2008 to 2010 shortly before the midterm elections. One of the key questions posed by our findings is whether the change in racial attitudes that we have outlined persisted. Thus, two years after the initial study, we went back into the field and recontacted a representative subsample of the initial panel participants. The central question we wanted to address was whether and to what extent the changes we observed during the campaign were sustained as both coverage of Obama and citizens' interest in politics waned after the election. Chapter 6 outlines the results of this examination and what they suggest about the long-term potential for prejudice reduction.

In the concluding chapter, we take a step back and consider the malleability of out-group attitudes and the ability of mass media to both reduce and encourage prejudice toward social out-groups. Ultimately, our findings underscore the modest pliability of racial attitudes and the ability of mass media to be a positive as well as a negative force for change. Because mass media are the primary source of ongoing exposure that many people have to those of different races, how they portray minorities matters a great deal.

Barack Obama's candidacy as the first black nominee of a major political party and his subsequent election as president of the United States represented important firsts in the history of the United States. Yet to date, most research on the 2008 presidential campaign supports a strictly pessimistic view, focusing on how white racial prejudice cost Obama votes. This perspective does not contradict any of our central findings. But on its own, it neglects the equally important effects of the Obama campaign *on* white racial attitudes. As evidenced by the civil rights movement in the 1960s, major national events have moved white racial attitudes in a more tolerant direction in the past. The 2008 Obama campaign may be merely the most recent such event. Our study lends a deeper understanding as to how such change comes about, how it might be sustained, and how it may revert without reinforcement.

Our approach to the study of racial attitudes in the 2008 election is very different from that of others who have focused on racial attitudes purely as an independent variable that influenced support for Obama. By contrast, we focus on racial attitudes strictly as a dependent variable that is susceptible to change as a result of this historic event. Importantly, we do not refute any arguments of previous scholars about whether America is "postracial," but neither do we consider this a serious question. By emphasizing change over time in racial attitudes, we do offer a somewhat less pessimistic assessment of the current and future state of race relations in the United States.

This study involves numerous methodological advantages in its examination of change over time. First and foremost is the fact that it is not just a time series reflecting similar aggregates over time, but a large, representative panel sample reflecting the views of over 2,500 white Americans over a six-month period. In addition, our novel statistical approach is uniquely well suited to studying change over time. Fixed-effects analyses of within-person change compare each person to himself or herself; this is useful because stable individual differences obviously cannot explain change over time that occurs within persons.[30] Thus, all potentially spurious causes of association that are due to unchanging characteristics of individuals—whether known or unknown—are accounted for by design and drop out of the model.[31] By contrast, the validity of most observational designs rests on the dubious assumption that one has perfectly measured, and explicitly controlled for, all potentially confounding characteristics.

Our approach also represents a substantial improvement over the older approach to panel analyses of employing lagged dependent variables.[32] Because lagged variables represent the stability of individual differences rather than a lack of change, their results can be misleading.[33] To be sure, fixed-effects models still leave open the possibility of spuriousness due to other variables that change over time and are not included in the model. By including a variable for each survey wave to represent the sheer passage of time, however, we are able to control for the sum total of all else that changed during the campaign.[34] This makes it unnecessary to include each and every time-varying variable in our models. Using three waves of panel data, we are able to provide the strongest possible causal evidence outside of a randomized experiment.[35]

On the one hand, no one doubts that the 2008 election was atypical in many respects. That the amount of coverage devoted to a single counter-stereotypical African American male by the American media was unprecedented may suggest that what we document in this book is sufficiently unusual that it is unlikely to ever happen again. On the other hand, by demonstrating that under these unusual circumstances whites' perceptions of blacks systematically changed, even in a relatively short period of time, our findings suggest that groups' perceptions of one another may be more malleable than previously thought. The fact that these perceptions became more positive during a time when economic conditions were clearly worsening only makes these changes more impressive. Negative white attitudes toward blacks may have less to do with any real-world competition than with the associations reinforced by what we see and hear every day.

PART I

Documenting Change in White Racial Attitudes During the 2008 Campaign

CHAPTER 2

Is the Decline in White Racial Prejudice Meaningful?

The intriguing finding presented in chapter 1 showed that, in the short span of the 2008 presidential campaign, white Americans became, on average, more positive in their views of African Americans. Here, before considering why this change occurred, we address several specific concerns that could undermine the significance of this change.

First, and most importantly: is what we measured really prejudice—that is, whites systematically favoring whites over blacks? A great deal has been written about the difficulties of tapping racial attitudes in America, so how do our measures stack up in this regard? Second, can we be certain that panel attrition does not threaten our evidence of this trend? The greater tendency of less racially progressive people to drop out of the study over time could mistakenly make it appear as if prejudice has declined. Third, we address the extent to which this change is, as we have predicted, a function of white attitudes toward blacks as opposed to changes in white attitudes toward their own in-group. Because in-group favoritism is a function of attitudes toward both the in-group and the out-group, we must disentangle these components to examine this question. Last, we address the breadth and magnitude of this trend. Is it widespread across social groups, or concentrated in a particular segment of the population? Relatively speaking, should we view it as small or large? We address each of these questions in turn.

IS WHAT WE MEASURED REALLY PREJUDICE?

Perhaps the most obvious alternative explanation for the decline in white racial prejudice is that whites simply became more likely to portray themselves as unprejudiced without actually changing their attitudes toward blacks. Indeed, immense controversy surrounds the measurement of racial prejudice in surveys, largely owing to concerns about social desirability bias.[1] In other words, is our measure confounded by the well-known tendency to present oneself in a more positive light to survey interviewers?

Many (though not all) white Americans are self-conscious about appearing racist. Suspicions about survey measures of racial prejudice began in the 1970s, when researchers noticed that despite a substantial drop in prejudice over the preceding decades, many whites remained steadfastly opposed to government efforts to reduce racial inequality.[2] Some researchers explained this "principle-implementation gap" by arguing that prejudice had not really declined so much as changed its stripes. In other words, whites no longer expressed racial prejudice in terms of blacks' inherent inferiority but rather in new, more subtle ways. Huge increases over the same time period in white support for the principle of racial equality indicated a sea change in social norms surrounding race—a demonstrably good thing, most agreed, yet one that researchers feared had made whites more likely to hide their remaining antiblack attitudes from survey interviewers.

From this school of thought arose a variety of measures designed to capture how whites really feel about blacks without the confounding influence of social desirability bias. One class of measures aims to assess "racial resentment," known variously as "modern," "symbolic," or "new" racism. Although the names of these measures vary, their conceptualization and operationalization overlap substantially. According to the theory underlying these measures, old-fashioned, or Jim Crow, racism has been replaced by a "subtle prejudice for modern times."[3] This "new racism" is theorized to be "a blend of anti-black affect and the kind of traditional American moral values embodied in the Protestant Ethic."[4] Whites may no longer believe that blacks are inherently inferior, but many whites still believe that blacks rely too much on government support rather than hard work. In other words, "persons who dislike blacks need only declare that they oppose government assistance to blacks not because they dislike them but because they believe in self-reliance."[5] "Today," Donald Kinder and Lynn Sanders argue, "prejudice is expressed in the language of individualism."[6]

Although prejudice certainly underlies the opposition of some whites to government programs to aid blacks, whites may also generally oppose such programs on politically conservative grounds, especially those who hold strong beliefs in individualism. Because the conceptualization and measurement of racial resentment assumes that individualism has become part of racial prejudice, these alternative explanations are extremely difficult to tease apart when using combined measures. Most studies use cross-sectional surveys to demonstrate significant associations between racial resentment and political attitudes while statistically controlling for political conservatism and/or beliefs in individualism.[7] However, the ability of these multivariate models to purge conservatism from indexes of racial resentment rests on the reliability with which the control variables are measured. Political conservatism is usually assessed with a single item, and the multi-item scale of beliefs in individualism unfortunately has low levels of reliability. Because racial resentment is measured with a highly reliable multi-item scale, the analyses are stacked in favor of finding a significant influence from racial resentment.[8]

Indeed, experimental evidence strongly suggests that measures of racial resentment are confounded with political conservatism and beliefs in individualism. One experiment varied the target of a government program so that the beneficiaries were alternatively blacks or whites and then examined the impact of racial resentment on program support among liberals and conservatives.[9] Among liberals, racial resentment decreased program support for blacks, but not program support for whites, just as one would expect if racial resentment taps prejudice against blacks. Among conservatives, however, racial resentment strongly influenced program support *regardless of the recipient's race.* Racial resentment appears, then, to successfully measure racial prejudice among liberals, but it also reflects nonracial values among conservatives.[10]

A second class of measures designed to avoid social desirability bias aims to assess "implicit" or "unconscious" racial prejudice, that is, attitudes held outside of conscious awareness.[11] Measures of implicit prejudice, like those of racial resentment, were created in response to the apparent decline in "old-fashioned" racism. But whereas racial resentment posits a new form of racism based on a combination of antiblack feelings and traditional moral values, theories of implicit prejudice posit "that racist attitudes remain prevalent but are buried in the unconscious."[12]

Of the many measures of implicit prejudice, the Implicit Association Test (IAT) is by far the most prominent.[13] The IAT compares the speed, or reaction times, with which people associate black and white names or faces with positively and negatively valenced words (for example, pleasant/unpleasant). When "a positive word following a white face is responded to more quickly by whites than is a positive word following an African-American face," this is said to demonstrate implicit prejudice.[14] Another popular implicit measure, the Affect Misattribution Procedure (AMP), presents an image of a black or white face followed by an image of a Chinese character, or ideograph.[15] Whites are told to disregard the image of the black or white face when evaluating the pleasantness of the Chinese ideograph, so when whites nonetheless give more negative evaluations of the Chinese ideographs following exposure to black faces, this is taken as evidence of implicit prejudice.

Measures of implicit prejudice clearly avoid social desirability biases. Because the IAT uses reaction-time tasks, faking responses is very difficult, if not impossible. The AMP, meanwhile, takes advantage of the well-known tendency for people to mistakenly attribute emotional responses from one stimuli to another. Nonetheless, a great deal of controversy surrounds the claim that implicit measures tap unconscious prejudice. As Hal Arkes and Philip Tetlock point out, "a person can be aware of cultural stereotypes, as indicated by the measure of implicit prejudice, but reject those same stereotypes."[16] Most everyone is aware of stereotypes linking blacks to criminality and poverty; hence, they might all reveal negative implicit associations with blacks. But whereas the truly prejudiced mostly attribute those stereotypes to the personal failings of blacks, the unprejudiced mostly attribute those stereotypes to ongoing discrimination and societal failures. Thus, implicit measures like the IAT and AMP are not clear indicators of prejudice, though they may well tap negative automatic associations.[17]

In any case, it remains unclear whether implicit measures provide any additional leverage for capturing the effects of prejudice on people's attitudes and behaviors beyond what we already know from self-report measures of prejudice. For instance, a study examining three nationally representative surveys showed no additional impact of implicit racial prejudice on vote choice in the 2008 presidential election after controlling for self-reported measures of racial prejudice and various demographic characteristics.[18] Moreover, the same study showed no consistent impact of implicit racial prejudice on racial policy attitudes after controlling for self-reported racial prejudice. Although other studies have shown significant associations between implicit racial prejudice and vote choice after controlling for self-reported measures of racial prejudice, those studies failed to control for party identification, political ideology, and other individual characteristics that could produce spurious associations.[19]

There are serious limitations to measures of racial resentment and implicit prejudice, so it is fortunate that we have at our disposal a measure of racial prejudice with a long history of uncontroversial use and the benefit of widespread agreement that it represents whites' tendency to favor their own racial group over blacks. This measure has appeared on two of the most widely used social science surveys, the General Social Survey (GSS) and the American National Election Studies (ANES), for more than two decades (since 1990 and 1992, respectively). Importantly, the measure does not directly query whites about their prejudices. Instead, the measure relies on questions that only indirectly assess the extent to which whites have more favorable attitudes toward whites than blacks.

Those familiar with the technique commonly used to tap ethnocentrism, a measure of generalized prejudice against others, will recognize this approach.[20] Ethnocentrism involves a combined assessment of several out-groups relative to a person's in-group. For example, Donald Kinder and Cindy Kam used items asking whites to rate their own in-group as well as blacks, Asians, and Hispanics on scales ranging from "hardworking" to "lazy," "intelligent" to "unintelligent," and "trustworthy" to "untrustworthy." In contrast to measures of ethnocentrism, this study draws strictly from positive and negative items asking about whites and blacks in order to assess white prejudice toward blacks.[21] By subtracting average favorability toward blacks from favorability toward whites, we created a measure of white racial prejudice.

Using the difference between ratings of blacks and whites on these items to construct a measure of racial prejudice is standard practice.[22] This is the case for a multitude of reasons. First, in-group favoritism produces discrimination even in the absence of out-group hostility.[23] Intergroup bias only requires that in-group members have *more* favorable views of their own in-group relative to the out-group. Second, to the extent that social desirability bias inflates ratings of the out-group, a measure of in-group favoritism can still detect prejudice so long as ratings of the in-group are even more positive. Third, and finally, there is a well-known tendency for survey respondents to rate groups positively or negatively across the board. So, for instance, a respondent's negative rating of blacks, Spencer Piston observes, "may be a reflection of her pessimistic view of people in general. . . . The difference measure therefore allows me to examine how a given respondent views blacks *relative* to whites."[24]

Thus, starting in the latter part of wave 3 (July 17 to August 29, 2008) and continuing through wave 4 (August 29 to November 4, 2008) and wave 5 (November 5, 2008, to January 31, 2009), a battery of six questions asked whites to rate both whites and blacks—with the order of presentation randomized independently in each wave—on three scales, ranging from "hardworking" to "lazy," "intelligent" to "unintelligent," and "trustworthy" to "untrustworthy." For each dimension, ratings of blacks were subtracted from ratings of whites, and then these difference scores were averaged.[25] Consistent with our assertion that these items tap a single underlying concept, the items were strongly intercorrelated, with Cronbach's alphas of 0.90 or higher on each wave.[26] In addition to demonstrating a very high reliability based on internal consistency, this measure also proved reliable using a much higher standard: true-score reliability using multi-wave panel data.[27] The measure of prejudice theoretically ranges from 0 to 100, but at least 95 percent of respondents in each panel wave had values in the range of 0 to 40.[28] Zero indicates an absence of in-group favoritism, and larger positive values indicate higher levels of prejudice. Because our interest was strictly in white prejudice against blacks, we recoded to 0 the small percentage of individual cases in which whites evaluated blacks more highly than whites.[29]

Although social desirability bias is always a potential concern with any self-report measure of racial prejudice, it appears unlikely to have altered people's responses in this case. To start, most whites gave prejudiced responses, as indicated by figure 1.1, which shows positive values on each and every day during the campaign and through Obama's inauguration. Clearly, racial prejudice is still "commonly expressed through stereotypes," as Kinder and Kam put it.[30] For instance, in the summer of 2008 (wave 3), fully 56 percent of whites showed favoritism for whites over blacks, suggesting that they had little aversion to answering in a way that indicated in-group favoritism, probably because our measure did not require whites to directly compare whites to blacks, as in measures of old-fashioned racism. Instead, whites evaluated their own group and evaluated blacks (with the order randomized) several minutes later (or earlier). As noted by Kinder and Kam, these types of "stereotype questions are formatted so that people can express favoritism for their own group without flagrantly violating norms of fairness. Thus, for example, white Americans who believe that blacks are less intelligent than whites can do so indirectly, in a sequence of separated judgments, without ever having to subscribe explicitly to the invidious comparison."[31] Moreover, even if some respondents wanted to appear unprejudiced by giving the same evaluations to both groups, several nonracial questions separated the two sets of items, presumably making it difficult to recall their previous answers. Making recall even more difficult was the fact that the points on the scales did not have labels other than the anchors on each end of the scales.

In addition, the survey was fielded over the Internet, which likely reduced the potential for social desirability bias substantially. Although plenty of evidence has revealed social desirability effects in response to racial attitude questions administered in face-to-face or telephone surveys, no evidence to date has shown such effects with Internet surveys.[32] Respondents have a greater sense of anonymity on Internet surveys because they answer the prejudice items without speaking to an interviewer (or even a computerized voice).

Nonetheless, as another check on potential social desirability effects, we used the randomized order of the items about whites and blacks to examine whether whites changed their evaluation of the second group to come closer to their evaluation of the previous one in an effort to rate the two groups more equally. If social desirability altered their responses, then whites should have evaluated blacks more positively when asked about them second (in order to match a putatively higher evaluation of the white in-group). Similarly, whites should have evaluated their own in-group less positively when blacks were asked about first (in order to match a putatively lower initial evaluation of the out-group). In neither case, however, was the pattern of results consistent with social desirability, nor did this pattern change over time. In fact, completely contrary to the expectation of social desirability bias, asking whites about their own in-group first produced *less* positive evaluations of blacks. And asking whites about blacks first produced *more* positive evaluations of whites.[33]

We also examined the decline in prejudice by level of education, another common way of assessing the impact of social desirability. Well-educated whites are more likely to know the "socially correct answers" on racial attitude questions—that is, to be sensitive to appearing unprejudiced.[34] Importantly, this cross-sectional difference would have no effect on a fixed-effects panel analysis of change over time: if a given individual exhibits the same degree of social desirability at all points in time, this bias will cancel itself out in panel analyses that compare the same person to himself or herself over time and thus would suggest no change over time in prejudice. As a result, social desirability bias alone cannot explain why people showed declines in racial prejudice during the 2008 campaign.

Figure 2.1   Change in White Racial Prejudice, by Level of Education,
July 17, 2008, to January 31, 2009

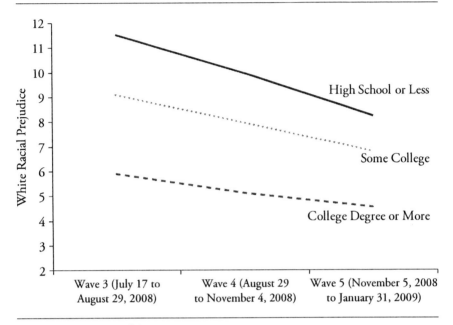

Source: 2008 NAES Panel Survey.
Note: A fixed-effects analysis predicting within-person change in prejudice from the wave 4 and 5 dummy variables (with wave 3 as the excluded reference category) and their interactions with education (in years) shows a positive and significant interaction between education and the wave 3 to 5 dummy variable (0.22, $p < .05$, N = 2,636), indicating a steeper decline among those with lower levels of education.

To the extent that the well-educated are also more sensitive to panel conditioning effects, however, whites could become increasingly more self-conscious about racial attitudes in later panel waves, thus leading to the appearance of lower prejudice scores. Did well-educated whites exhibit larger declines in racial prejudice? As shown in figure 2.1, racial prejudice declined significantly more among whites with *lower* levels of education.[35] In other words, racial prejudice declined the most among those presumably least sensitive to social desirability and panel conditioning.

Unfortunately, panel conditioning is a broader problem than can be examined through educational comparisons alone. Whenever merely answering a question on one wave influences responses on later survey waves, panel conditioning is potentially problematic. In this study, panel conditioning could be especially problematic if it indicated that whites became increasingly self-conscious about how they answered the racial prejudice items. For this reason, we conducted additional analyses using as independent variables the number of prior survey waves in which whites had participated and the number of months that a respondent had been a part of the GfK (formerly Knowledge Networks) panel.[36] Demographic and political variables were included to control for attrition. The number of prior waves in which a respondent participated had no effect on levels of racial prejudice. Specifically, using OLS regression predicting wave 5 prejudice, we found no significant effects from the number of prior waves in which a respondent had participated that included the prejudice items $(-0.30, p = 0.18, N = 14,229)$. Moreover, we found the same null result if we instead used the number of prior waves with *any* items concerning race.

Although social desirability bias does not appear to be a concern for our central measure, one might still wonder if alternative measures of racial prejudice, such as measures of implicit prejudice or racial resentment, would have revealed the same decline in prejudice during the campaign. At least in political contexts, measures of implicit racial prejudice do not appear to capture unique variance above and beyond measures of explicit racial prejudice. For example, implicit racial prejudice had no impact on vote choice in the 2008 election after controlling for explicit racial prejudice and standard demographics.[37] More to the point, a laboratory experiment conducted after the campaign found that exposure to Obama reduced levels of racial prejudice on an implicit measure of prejudice, consistent with the exemplification mechanism underlying our theory of mediated intergroup contact.[38]

Another popular measure, racial resentment, is strongly correlated with the measure of racial prejudice used in this study, and both measures have similar correlations with race-related policy attitudes.[39] A recent study by Nicholas Valentino and Ted Brader appears to contradict our findings of decreasing prejudice, but in fact their results reinforce our findings.[40] Despite the much shorter time frame of their panel survey, which was fielded immediately before and after the election, there was a significant overall *decline* in racial resentment among the sample as a whole.[41]

Taken together, we are very confident that what we measured is in fact racial prejudice. One may argue with our use of the term "prejudice," but it is consistent with numerous scholarly studies. Lawrence Bobo and James Kluegel used these items to create a "Prejudice Index [that] measures racial stereotyping of the type commonly included in definitions of 'anti-black prejudice.'"[42] Along similar lines, Donald Kinder and Cindy Kam have more recently employed these items to assess "generalized prejudice" or "ethnocentrism"—that is, in-group favoritism relative to out-group opinions.[43] Perhaps more importantly, regardless of what we call it, this measure has undeniably important consequences in that it predicts support for public policies and evaluations of individual African Americans.[44]

IS THE DECLINE IN PREJUDICE DUE TO PANEL ATTRITION?

Panel attrition occurs when some people who participated in one wave of a survey do not participate in subsequent waves. All panel studies experience attrition, and on its own, this is not a problem for our ability to make inferences about the general population. But to the extent that attrition is systematic rather than random, it can produce an unrepresentative panel sample and an unrealistic estimate, in this case, of the size of the decline in racial prejudice.

Did panel attrition make our sample substantially unrepresentative of the general population? On the contrary, our sample was broadly representative of the population. Although respondents answered the surveys via the Internet, respondents with and without Internet access were recruited using random digit–dialing and address-based sampling. Importantly, participants without regular Internet access were provided with a laptop and free access. Because most of our analyses rely on the sample of non-Hispanic whites who completed waves 3, 4, and 5, we compared this sample to the July 2008 Current Population Survey (CPS), carried out by the U.S. Census Bureau. Following standard procedure, we compared the samples in terms of gender, income, age, and education.[45] On gender and income, the two samples were strikingly similar. Sixteen percent of whites in the CPS and 13 percent of whites in our sample had annual incomes of $25,000 or less, and 48 percent of whites in both samples identified as male. As is typical of national surveys, younger whites were somewhat underrepresented, with 18 percent of whites on the CPS and 6 percent of whites in our sample falling into the eighteen- to twenty-nine-year-old bracket. Along similar lines, our sample underrepresented those with the least education, with 40 percent of whites in the CPS and 22 percent of whites in our sample having a high school degree or less.

Did panel attrition thus bias our estimates of the extent of change in racial prejudice? Fortunately, to the extent that *selective* attrition did occur, it probably led to underestimates of the size of the decline in racial prejudice. Selective attrition was predictably concentrated among less-educated whites. As shown in figure 2.1, racial prejudice declined *more* among the less-educated, so underrepresentation of this group ought to have produced underestimates of the overall decline in racial prejudice. The less-educated also tend to have higher levels of prejudice. The loss of less-educated whites through attrition biased downward the levels of initial prejudice in our sample; thus, our estimates of the size of the decline in prejudice during the campaign were also biased downward. Consistent with this possibility, among all whites in wave 3, the mean level of prejudice was 8.48, whereas whites who dropped out after wave 3 had a mean level of prejudice of 9.18, a significant difference ($p < 0.001$). In addition, the decline in racial prejudice did not vary significantly by age, so underrepresentation of the youngest age group probably had little or no impact on our estimates of the size of the decline in racial prejudice (see table 2.1).

Given the impossibility of perfectly representative samples, many survey researchers use post-stratification weights to make their samples look more like the census distributions on the handful of demographic characteristics included in the CPS (age, gender, income, education, and race and ethnicity). On the one hand, the ability to make one's sample look more representative of the general population has obvious appeal when the goal is to make inferences about the general population. On the other hand, weighting sacrifices statistical power. We have no firm position on this issue, nor does it turn out to be important to most of our analyses. We have opted to present unweighted results throughout the book, but we have replicated all of our analyses using weights, and we note any cases where doing so significantly alters our results.

IS THE DECLINE IN PREJUDICE DUE TO A CHANGE IN ATTITUDES TOWARD WHITES RATHER THAN ATTITUDES TOWARD BLACKS?

Although it is clear that white racial prejudice declined over the course of the campaign, it is unclear whether this occurred because whites evaluated blacks more favorably by the end of the campaign or because whites evaluated whites less favorably. If our theory is correct—if exposure to Obama caused whites to change their attitudes toward blacks as a group—then the decline in racial prejudice should have resulted primarily from changes in attitudes toward blacks.

Figure 1.1 shows aggregate shifts in the gap between whites' perceptions of blacks and whites, but it does not provide an appropriate statistical test. Before examining our prejudice measure's separate components, we first establish the statistical significance of this decline. To assess whether whites significantly changed their attitudes toward blacks and whites over the course of the 2008 campaign, we employ fixed-effects panel regression models, which compare

Table 2.1   White Racial Prejudice by Panel Wave
             and Population Subgroup

	Wave 3	Wave 4	Wave 5	Change from Wave 3 to Wave 5
Overall sample	8.16	7.10	6.09	−2.07***
Education				
High school or less	11.54	9.98	8.25	−3.29***
Some college	9.10	7.96	6.81	−2.29***
BA degree or more	5.91	5.13	4.56	−1.35***
Age				
Youngest third	7.82	6.70	5.98	−1.84***
Middle third	7.32	6.37	5.33	−1.99***
Oldest third	9.14	8.01	6.81	−2.33***
Region				
South	9.82	9.27	8.23	−1.59**
Non-South	7.54	6.27	5.27	−2.27***
Gender				
Male	8.69	7.64	6.88	−1.81***
Female	7.69	6.60	5.37	−2.32***
Income				
Lower half	9.24	8.12	7.31	−1.93***
Upper half	7.45	6.42	5.27	−2.18***
Vote Intention				
McCain voter	10.97	9.95	8.19	−2.78***
Obama voter	4.56	3.66	3.52	−0.90***
Party Identification				
Republican	10.70	9.48	7.87	−2.83***
Independent	7.19	6.15	4.98	−2.21***
Democrat	6.25	5.34	5.34	−0.91*
Ideology				
Conservative	9.83	8.89	7.16	−2.67***
Moderate	9.14	7.18	6.47	−2.67***
Liberal	4.26	4.07	3.81	−0.45

Source: 2008 NAES Panel Survey.
Note: The total sample size is 2,636, except for the analyses involving vote intention (N = 2,192) and ideology (N = 2,583). To assess whether the means in waves 3 and 5 differ significantly within subgroups we used paired t-tests (two-tailed).
***$p < 0.001$; **$p < 0.01$; * $p < 0.05$

Table 2.2   Within-Person Change in White Racial Prejudice, Attitudes Toward Blacks, and Attitudes Toward Whites

	White Racial Prejudice	Attitudes Toward Blacks	Attitudes Toward Whites
Time			
Wave 3 to wave 4	−1.07***	2.28***	1.53***
	(0.22)	(0.35)	(0.34)
Wave 3 to wave 5	−2.08***	1.74***	−0.09
	(0.22)	(0.35)	(0.34)
Constant	9.54***	3.04***	11.53***
	(0.35)	(0.57)	(0.56)
Sample size	2,636	2,636	2,636

Source: 2008 NAES Panel Survey.
Note: The table presents unstandardized fixed-effects regression coefficients, with standard errors in parentheses. Each column presents a different fixed-effects model and also controls for the order in which the racial groups (in-group and out-group) were asked about.
***$p < 0.001$

each individual respondent to himself or herself at an earlier point in time.[46] Thus, unlike cross-sectional analyses, which compare different individuals at a single point in time, fixed-effects models of within-person change assess the extent to which each individual changed his or her attitudes over time. When these models include no other independent variables, the wave coefficients indicate how much total average change has occurred between pairs of waves.[47]

Using a fixed-effects model, table 2.2 first confirms that white racial prejudice declined significantly over time at the individual level. As shown in model 1, both the wave 3 to 4 and the wave 3 to 5 dummy variables indicate a significant decline in prejudice. Specifically, the coefficient of −1.07 for the wave 3 to 4 dummy variable indicates that prejudice declined, on average, by about one point from wave 3 to wave 4. The coefficient of −2.08 for the wave 3 to 5 dummy variable indicates that prejudice declined, on average, by two points from wave 3 to wave 5.

Was this decline driven by a positive shift in attitudes toward blacks or a negative shift in attitudes toward whites? As shown in model 2 of table 2.2, consistent with our theory, attitudes toward blacks show a significant positive change from wave 3 to wave 4 of 2.28 points on average. From wave 3 to wave 5, however, we see a positive change of just 1.74 points, on average, implying that attitudes toward blacks became slightly less positive from wave 4 to wave 5. Importantly for our theory, attitudes toward blacks remained far more positive in wave 5 relative to wave 3. Given that attention to Obama peaked in wave 4 and dropped off substantially after the election (see chapter 6 for details), it makes sense that attitudes toward blacks improved the most between waves 3 and 4 and then declined to a smaller extent when attention to Obama faded after the election.

In contrast to the possibility that in-group favoritism declined because whites became more negative toward their own in-group, model 3 of table 2.2 shows a significant positive change in attitudes toward whites from wave 3 to wave 4 (1.53, $p < 0.001$) and no change from wave 3 to wave 5 ($-.09$, $p > 0.10$). By the end of the campaign, whites held the same views of their in-group as they had held at the beginning of the campaign. Taken together, the results in table 2.2 indicate that the primary driver of the decline in racial prejudice during the 2008 campaign was a positive shift in attitudes toward the black out-group, not a trend toward more negative views of the white in-group. Just as mediated intergroup contact predicted, it was whites' views of blacks that changed, not their views of whites.

DID PREJUDICE DECLINE AMONG THOSE FOR WHOM IT MATTERED LEAST?

Our analyses thus far give us great confidence that white racial prejudice did in fact decline during the 2008 campaign, driven by a positive change in whites' images of African Americans. But it is still possible that these shifts were confined to whites who were less prejudiced to begin with—that is, those who were least in need of changing their views.

In a political campaign, opposing partisans strenuously resist the messages coming from the other side. For this reason, there is a tendency to think that predictions regarding the effects of a positive exemplar on racial attitudes should follow a similar pattern. In other words, only those with already positive views of Obama, and perhaps those with weakly held political views, should be subject to influence.

This assumption neglects an important difference between theories of political persuasion and the process of exemplification. Mediated intergroup contact via exemplification is believed to operate through a passive psychological process, below individuals' level of conscious awareness. Because this process operates below the radar, resistance to counterstereotypical portrayals of blacks should be minimized. People who are not aware that their associations are being altered have no way to consciously resist that change. Whereas conservatives surely resisted Obama's explicit political appeals, the countless images of Obama

Figure 2.2   Change in White Racial Prejudice, by Vote Intention

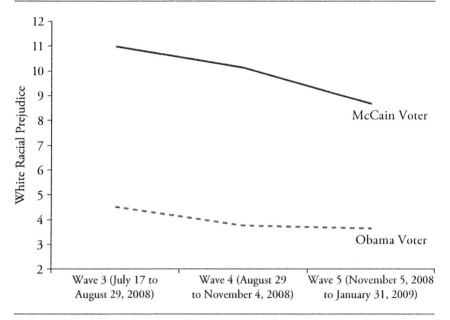

Source: 2008 NAES Panel Survey.
Note: Vote intention was assessed on wave 3, where 0 equals support for Obama and 1 equals support for McCain. A fixed-effects model of within-person change reveals a negative and statistically significant interaction between vote intention and the wave 3 to 5 dummy variable (-1.72, $p < 0.001$, N = 2,192).

to which they were exposed refuted stereotypes implicitly, thus operating without their conscious awareness. In fact, because conservatives have higher initial levels of prejudice, exemplification theory predicts larger reductions in their prejudice because Obama was likely to differ from their expectations of blacks more than he did for those with less initial prejudice. Any altering of whites' implicit associations and how they think about blacks more generally would be unlikely in a context where this was the obvious persuasive goal. Under those circumstances, it would be all too easy to dismiss Obama as the exception, as predicted by subtyping theory, a topic explored more thoroughly in chapter 4.

To examine whether racial prejudice declined more among Obama's political opponents or his political supporters, we tested for interactions between individuals' political predispositions and the wave variables in our fixed-effects models.[48] We measured support for Obama in three ways: pre-election vote intention, ideology, and party identification. Figure 2.2 shows the extent to

Figure 2.3   Change in White Racial Prejudice, by Political Ideology

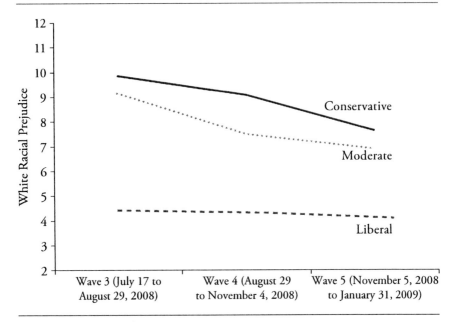

Source: 2008 NAES Panel Survey.
Note: Political ideology was measured on wave 3 or in a previous wave. A fixed-effects model of within-person change with dummy variables for moderates and conservatives (with liberals as the excluded category) yields negative and significant interactions between the moderate and conservative dummy variables and the wave 3 to 5 dummy variable (–2.14 and –2.13, respectively, $p < 0.001$, N = 2,583).

which change over time in white racial prejudice varied by vote intention. Clearly, prejudice declined to a much greater extent among McCain supporters than among Obama supporters. Confirming this impression, a fixed-effects model of within-person change revealed a negative and statistically significant interaction between vote intention and the wave 3 to 5 dummy variable.

The results when using political ideology or party identification to identify those predisposed to like Obama told the same story. As shown in figure 2.3, prejudice declined substantially more among conservatives and moderates than among liberals. A fixed-effects model of within-person change with dummy variables for moderates and conservatives (with liberals as the excluded category) confirmed the statistical significance of these differential changes, yielding negative and significant interactions between the dummies for moderates

Figure 2.4   Change in White Racial Prejudice, by Party Identification

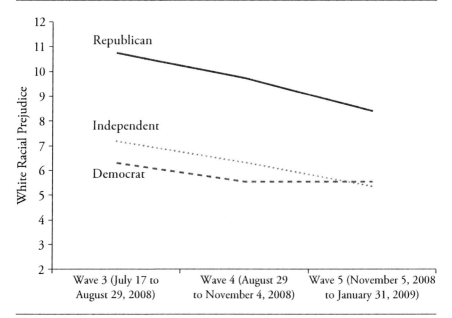

Source: 2008 NAES Panel Survey.
Note: Party identification was measured on wave 3 or in a previous wave. A fixed-effects model of within-person change yields negative and significant interactions between dummy variables representing Republicans and independents (with Democrats as the excluded reference category) and the wave 3 to 5 dummy variable (-1.90, $p < 0.01$ and -1.26, $p < 0.05$, respectively, N = 2,636).

and conservatives and the wave 3 to 5 dummy variable (-2.14 and -2.13, respectively, $p < 0.001$, N = 2,583).

Finally, figure 2.4 shows a similar pattern using party identification, with larger declines in prejudice among Republicans and independents than among Democrats. Again, these differential changes over time are statistically significant. The model yielded negative and significant interactions between dummy variables representing Republicans and independents (with Democrats as the excluded reference category) and the wave 3 to 5 dummy variable (-1.90, $p < 0.01$, and -1.26, $p < 0.05$, respectively, N = 2,636).

Importantly, these patterns were not due to regression to the mean, which would imply random fluctuations between each pair of waves. Between waves 3 and 4, this would have meant a *decrease* in prejudice among those with high initial levels of prejudice and an *increase* in prejudice among those with low initial levels of prejudice. Between waves 4 and 5, the two groups would have either shown no change or reverted back toward their initial values (that is, they would have regressed back to their group means). But instead of such random fluctuations, a systematic pattern emerged: those with high initial levels of prejudice exhibited *consistent* declines in prejudice across both pairs of waves, and even those with low initial levels of prejudice exhibited small declines. Consistent with a theory of mediated intergroup contact, white racial prejudice declined the most among whites with higher initial prejudice, including McCain supporters, Republicans, and conservatives.

Perhaps surprisingly, changes in racial attitudes were also fairly widespread. As shown in table 2.1, prejudice declined significantly among both younger and older whites, men and women, the wealthy and the poor, and even among Southerners as well as those living outside the South. In fact, we found no evidence of differential change by age, gender, income, or region. The overall homogeneity of effects was noteworthy given the amount of attention these demographic categories receive in the literature on race. Given the prominence of young people as supporters of Obama, one might have expected the declines in prejudice to be limited to this subgroup. Along similar lines, news coverage emphasized Obama's problems in attracting men and members of the working class. Although these social cleavages may be relevant predictors of vote choice, they are irrelevant as predictors of within-person change in racial attitudes. These results may surprise scholars who are accustomed to comparing levels of prejudice across groups at a single point in time. However, these patterns underscore the benefits of panel data for shedding light on the more interesting and useful question of what predicts *change* over time in racial attitudes.

IS THE DECLINE IN PREJUDICE SMALL?

Although our findings suggest that the statistically significant decline in racial prejudice is widespread, the size of the decline is of obvious importance as well. The question of whether a decline is considered small or large is inevitably subjective, but it is probably best answered by considering how much racial prejudice typically changes during the time period of a campaign. The literature on racial prejudice suggests that it is a highly stable characteristic, changing little from year to year.[49] In recent years, levels of racial prejudice have not changed much at all.[50] Thus, any significant change during the short six-month span of a presidential campaign would be unusual.

Fortunately, we can evaluate the relative amount of change in 2008 directly because the same measure of racial prejudice that we used has been included, as mentioned earlier, on the General Social Survey and the American National Election Studies for two decades. The ANES is fielded every four years around the presidential election, while the GSS is fielded every two years. Neither of these surveys involves panel data on racial attitudes, but they allow us to examine whether the decline in racial prejudice during the 2008 campaign was large or small by historical standards—that is, relative to recent secular trends.[51]

Specifically, we compared the extent of change in prejudice during the 2008 campaign with the year-to-year historical fluctuations on the GSS and ANES. Because the response scales on the items differ across the GSS, ANES, and our panel survey, we standardized the prejudice scores. Given that our panel covered approximately a six-month period, we calculated the amount of change (whether in a positive or negative direction) per six-month period on the ANES and GSS. In other words, we calculated the absolute value of the differences between each pair of adjacent surveys, summed the differences, and then divided by the number of six-month periods covered by each time series. Note that we did not simply subtract the prejudice score from the earliest time period from the score for the most recent time period on the GSS and ANES, but instead calculated the differences between each pair of adjacent surveys.

As shown in figure 2.5, the extent of change in racial prejudice during the 2008 campaign was substantial relative to recent historical fluctuations. Racial prejudice changed by 0.14 standard deviations during the six months of the 2008 campaign, relative to just 0.03 standard deviations, on average, per six-month period over the eighteen years covered by the GSS. Similarly, over the sixteen years covered by the ANES, prejudice changed by only 0.01 standard deviations, on average, per six-month period. By this metric, the decline in racial prejudice during the 2008 campaign was huge, a rate of decline between five and fourteen times faster than the secular decline in prejudice over the previous two decades. Although we cannot say in any precise sense what is large enough to be considered "meaningful," relative to recent historical standards, the size of the change during the Obama campaign was large.

A SYSTEMATIC AND SIZABLE CHANGE

We began this chapter with an intriguing finding: during the short span of the 2008 presidential campaign, white racial prejudice declined. Yet many additional questions needed to be answered before we could be convinced

Figure 2.5   Standardized Change in White Racial Prejudice per
               Six-Month Period, 1990 to 2008 and During the
               2008 Campaign

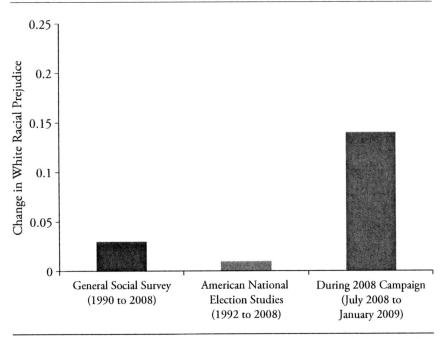

Source: 1990–2008 General Social Surveys, 1992–2008 American National Election Studies, 2008 NAES Panel Survey.

of the significance of this trend. The number-one concern of public opinion researchers studying race is social desirability bias: do whites hide their real views in order to appear less racist? Given how strong social norms against racism are in America today, the potential for social desirability bias is strong. Knowing this, we designed our study to minimize socially desirable responses and, critically, to allow us to examine whether we had succeeded. Based on the variety of tests described in this chapter, we are confident that the decline in prejudice is real and not based on increased sensitivity to questions pertaining to race. The best evidence of this is, ironically, that most white Americans gave prejudiced responses on all three waves of the survey, despite showing significant reductions in prejudice over time.

We also ruled out two potential alternative explanations for the decline stemming from the panel design of the survey. First we asked whether the changes in racial attitudes were spurred by panel conditioning—that is, did the act of answering the survey itself, responding to questions about blacks, make whites self-conscious about their racial attitudes? Fortunately, having designed the study to test this proposition directly, we found no evidence for it. The number of prior waves in the survey that whites participated in had no effect on later responses. Setting aside panel conditioning, however, it remained possible that panel attrition had skewed our sample. If the respondents who dropped out of the study between waves were substantially different from those who stayed in the study, this could have made the sample unrepresentative and limited our ability to generalize about white Americans. Here we benefited from unusually low levels of attrition. In addition, the composition of the dropouts worked *against* finding reductions in racial prejudice, thus bolstering our sense that the changes we documented are real.

With panel conditioning and attrition set aside, we directly addressed the theory of mediated intergroup contact via exemplification. In-group favoritism may decline based on either an improvement in views of the out-group or a tempering of enthusiasm for the in-group. Yet we presupposed that whites had changed their views of the out-group, rather than that they had become less prejudiced because they had lowered their views of their own white in-group. Our evidence clearly supports the expectation of mediated intergroup contact. The decline in white racial prejudice was driven primarily by a positive shift in attitudes toward blacks.

Further, we examined expectations specific to the theory. Counter to conventional wisdom in political science, the theory predicted that prejudice would decline the most among whites with higher initial levels of prejudice, including McCain voters, Republicans, and conservatives. Unlike political persuasion as traditionally understood, exemplification, the unique psychological process underlying mediated contact, is a passive, unconscious process. Campaign coverage of Obama was not overtly about changing white attitudes toward African Americans. The campaign, on its face, was about politics and policy. But while viewers focused their conscious attention on the campaign, they were nonetheless exposed to a deluge of counterstereotypical portrayals of Obama and his family. This type of psychological process minimizes resistance based on preexisting attitudes. Indeed, it promotes change *especially* among those with more negative preexisting attitudes because these are the people for whom the counterstereotypical portrayals most strongly counter their initial impressions of the out-group. Consistent with this theory, prejudice declined the most among whites with higher initial prejudice—namely, McCain voters, Republicans, and conservatives—though prejudice declined among Obama's supporters as well. Indeed, the overarching message of our findings is that racial prejudice declined across the board, regardless of age, gender, income, education, or region of residence.

Not only was the decline in prejudice broad-based, but it was also large by historical standards. We relied on historical precedent to help us interpret how large a change in prejudice would have been substantial in light of recent history. Whether the amount of change should be considered "a little" or "a lot" depends on one's expectations of how prejudice typically changes in the absence of an intervening event. Based on our analyses, levels of racial prejudice move very little, on average, during typical six-month periods. By comparison, racial prejudice declined by a huge amount during the 2008 campaign.

None of this is to say that racial prejudice has disappeared, of course. But a substantial change to an otherwise stubborn predisposition has taken place. The decline in racial prejudice is undoubtedly meaningful and worthy of exploration and explanation.

CHAPTER 3

Visions of Unity: White Perceptions of Race Relations

Few people who witnessed the inauguration of Barack Hussein Obama on January 20, 2009, could mistake the momentous nature of the day's events, nor the jubilant mood of the participants, black and white alike. Likewise, the *Washington Post* (November 8, 2008) described election night as "Rapture in the Streets as Multitudes Cheer Obama and Celebrate America."[1] The sight of this event caused both white and black children to reevaluate who could actually grow up to be president someday; indeed, these inspirational effects had become evident long before the election, when Obama became the first black nominee of a major political party.[2]

Not surprisingly, all the available sources of data show that people's perceptions of race relations improved during this period.[3] What is perhaps most surprising is the ambivalence with which this evidence has been received. For the most part, this conciliatory trend has been deemed bad news by academic observers. However, as we demonstrate in this chapter, these reactions stem from either misunderstandings of the consequences of perceived improvements in race relations or a concern for maintaining affirmative action above all else.

We begin with an overview of what our panel study suggests about perceptions of race relations during the 2008 campaign. Next, we turn to auxiliary analyses that help us examine what this trend meant for both blacks and whites. Finally, we present several arguments as to why improved perceptions of race relations are a positive development for blacks and whites, and we also respond to arguments that have deemed such improvement a mixed blessing at best.

To date, trends in perceptions of race relations have not been widely studied by academics, although they have been featured regularly in the press releases of news organizations. The academic literature has probably neglected these perceptions because they are indeed just that: *perceptions*, with no relationship necessarily to reality. As a result, it is not clear precisely what one should make of them. The popular press generally heralds improvements in perceptions of race relations as a positive development. Even in the sparse academic literature addressing perceptions of race relations, there are some who view perceptions of improvement as a desirable trend because they are indicative of lower levels of intergroup tension. But as we explain in this chapter, this interpretation is not universally shared. Regardless of one's perspective on this change, ongoing perceptions of race relations have drawn greater public scrutiny in the wake of Obama's election.

TRENDS IN PERCEPTIONS OF RACE RELATIONS DURING 2008

From April 2008 through the inauguration in January 2009, respondents in our panel survey were asked three questions about race relations: one addressed the current state of race relations, another tapped the extent of perceived improvement over the last ten years, and the third tapped the respondent's level of optimism or pessimism about race relations over the next ten years. With an event of the magnitude of Obama's nomination as the first African American candidate from a major party—and later his election as the first African American president—one would be surprised if perceptions of race relations did not improve. Indeed, as shown in figure 3.1, whites' perceptions of the past, present, and future of race relations all became rosier over the course of the 2008 presidential election. With zero on the vertical axis representing perceptions of no change, positive scores representing perceived improvement, and negative scores representing decline, it is clear that, overall, perceptions became more positive and optimistic. The trend lines for change over the *last* ten years and anticipated change over the *next* ten years are virtually identical, both in absolute levels of optimism and in the slope of the upward trend over time. As can be seen in figure 3.1, perceptions of both the past and future gradually shifted in a more positive direction throughout the election year.

Figure 3.1   Change in White Perceptions of Race Relations over the Last Ten Years, Today, and over the Next Ten Years

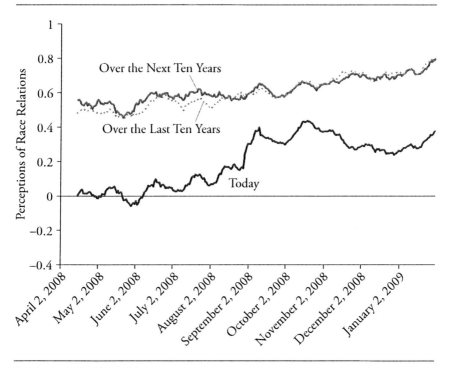

Source: 2008 NAES Panel Survey.

Note: Each measure of perceptions of race relations relies on a five-point scale that ranges from −2 to 2, where negative values indicate a pessimistic view, 0 equals a neutral view, and positive values indicate an optimistic view of race relations. The sample sizes for perceptions of race relations over the last ten years are 15,699 for wave 3, 15,247 for wave 4, and 15,300 for wave 5. The sample sizes for perceptions of race relations today are 15,727 for wave 3, 15,295 for wave 4, and 15,313 for wave 5. The sample sizes for perceptions of race relations over the next ten years are 15,665 for wave 3, 15,219 for wave 4, and 15,278 for wave 5.

Interestingly, perceptions of race relations *today* stand out as systematically more negative than those in the past and future, although the overall slope is still positive. But quite logically, perceptions of current race relations also tend to be much more variable over time, because assessments of the present will invariably change over shorter periods of time as events unfold. In addition, a large jump in more positive perceptions of race relations today, but not optimism about the past or future, occurred on August 28, 2008, the day Obama accepted the Democratic nomination.

Overall, the positive change in perceptions was highly statistically significant, with the vast majority of improvement in perceived race relations occurring before Obama was actually elected, that is, between the pre-election waves. The pattern suggests that a general positivity infused assessments of past, present, and future race relations. To be clear, we do not interpret these positive trends as evidence that a large number of concrete changes in race relations actually occurred during the campaign. Indeed, the fact that people responded in roughly the same ways regardless of whether they were asked about the past ten years, the present, or the next ten years suggests that these views are not rooted in empirical observations or real-world experiences. Nothing that happened during the campaign should have substantially changed a person's assessment of the past ten years, nor did the campaign hand people prognostications of the future. We assume that what these items are tapping is an overall positive mood with respect to race relations, and this positive mood at least temporarily infused assessments of past, present, and future. Because these three measures of perceived race relations were also highly intercorrelated for individuals at any given point in time (Cronbach's alpha averaged 0.72 across the three waves), we treat them as a single index of perceived race relations in our subsequent analyses.

How should we interpret the evidence in figure 3.1? First, it is unclear whether whites' perceptions of improvement meant that blacks also perceived race relations as improving. For this reason, whites' perceptions are typically compared to blacks' perceptions to see whether a trend toward more optimistic sentiment is at least shared by both races. Clearly, if whites perceive race relations to be improving but blacks do not, whites' perceptions of improvement would be cast in a very different light. Such a pattern would suggest that whites are once again oblivious to ongoing racial tensions. But if blacks perceive race relations to be better as well, then our confidence in the idea that this trend represents an actual lessening of racial tensions should increase, because it suggests that whites and blacks are on the same page.

In figure 3.2, we illustrate trends for the index comprising the three items that assess race relations in the past, present, and future, this time showing the overall trend for both blacks and whites. A quick glance at figure 3.2 makes it clear that both blacks and whites became more optimistic about race relations during the 2008 election. The variability in estimates for blacks is greater owing to their smaller numbers in the sample. Nonetheless, blacks went from being predominantly negative about race relations to predominantly positive during this short span of a few months. Moreover, blacks' perceptions of race

Figure 3.2   Change in White and Black Perceptions
of Race Relations

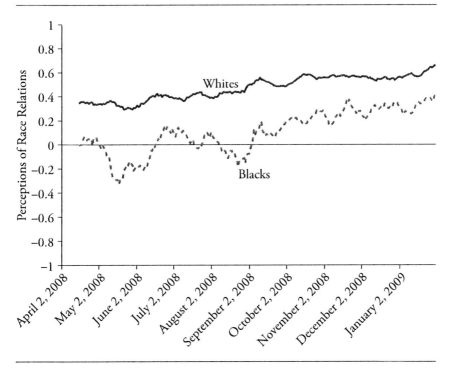

Source: 2008 NAES Panel Survey.
Note: Perceptions of race relations were assessed using a scale of three items measuring perceptions of race relations today, over the last ten years, and over the next ten years. The scale ranges from −2 to 2, where negative values indicate a pessimistic view, 0 equals a neutral view, and positive values indicate an optimistic view of race relations. Among whites, the sample size for wave 3 is 15,765; for wave 4, 15,323; and for wave 5, 15,365. Among blacks, the sample size for wave 3 is 1,878; for wave 4, 1,745; and for wave 5, 1,671.

relations improved to a significantly greater extent than whites' perceptions of race relations. Overall, blacks' perceptions of improvement were twice the magnitude of whites' perceptions of improvement in race relations. Clearly, when it comes to perceptions of race relations, both blacks and whites responded to the Obama campaign in similar ways. Both groups *perceived* substantial improvement in race relations during the Obama campaign.

We have highlighted the fact that other than Obama's campaign, nothing particularly momentous happened during this time period that seems likely to have changed the perceived relationship between blacks and whites on a large scale. But to characterize the changes in racial prejudice that we have observed as "merely" symbolic or as reflective of an amorphous and inconsequential era of good feelings is to undercut the importance of what transpired even before Obama was elected. Indeed, the historical and symbolic value of Obama's campaign and election is frequently "brushed aside," David Hollinger observes, "amid a competition over who can declare the most resoundingly that racism is still a vital problem in the United States."[4] No one seriously argues that the United States has erased the legacy of racism because of Obama's election. And yet there is a sense among many academic observers that to stop and enjoy the moment—even bask in it—is to deny the existence of racial inequality and court the possibility of bad things happening as a result. Thus, many academics recoil at headlines such as the one on the *New York Times* front page the day after the election, which proclaimed in self-congratulatory fashion, "Take a Bow, America." As the *Times* put it, "The multiracial crowds dancing with unrestrained joy from coast to coast on Tuesday night were proof that the promise of America lives—and that you can't always hang your hat on logic."[5]

Racial inequality between blacks and whites did not suddenly disappear because a black president was elected. Indeed, even if *all* prejudicial attitudes and beliefs were to magically disappear overnight, it would not produce racial equality. But likewise, even the instantaneous appearance of economic equality between the races would not automatically eliminate prejudicial attitudes toward blacks and white in-group favoritism. Our point is that to insist that the only worthwhile goals are either racial equality or the combination of racial equality with the elimination of racial prejudice is to overlook the interdependence of these problems. Indeed, the whole point of the social construction of "African Americans" as a distinct, stigmatized subgroup was economic exploitation.[6] Economic inequality and prejudice feed off of one another, with the relatively poor economic position of blacks feeding prejudicial views of this group, and prejudicial views feeding that inequality.

Anything that cuts into this negative cycle by either reducing prejudice or improving the economic status of blacks is to be lauded, but neither prejudice reduction nor improvement in blacks' economic status is an acceptable substitute for the other. Reducing negative perceptions of white-black difference is precisely what the flood of coverage of Obama's campaign accomplished. As a black engineer described it, "It's like this new 'a-ha' moment for them [whites] . . . finding out that some of the goals that we of color try to attain are similar to theirs."[7]

A DOWNSIDE OF IMPROVED PERCEPTIONS OF RACE RELATIONS?

When perceptions of race relations improve—particularly when they improve among both blacks and whites—pundits and the press typically herald this as good news. As *USA Today* suggested during the campaign, in response to such findings, "Hopes for Race Relations Are High."[8] A shift toward more positive perceptions is popularly deemed a healthy development. But interestingly, this was not the case among many academics observing the same trend during the 2008 election period. To assess these rival arguments, we first attempt to anchor perceptions of race relations to something more tangibly important, such as prejudice, that is, the extent to which whites evaluate their white in-group more favorably than blacks.

Instead of serving as a bellwether of welcome changes in interracial relations, improved perceptions of the extent of racial discrimination have been deemed as at best a "double-edged sword," as Nicholas Valentino and Ted Brader put it.[9] The rationale for this interpretation is that a decline in perceptions of discrimi-nation may reduce support for policies designed to redress past effects of racial discrimination. Valentino and Brader argue that any issues for which opinions are "racialized" should produce effects of this kind.

The logic behind this prediction is obvious: a policy designed to correct past racial inequities, such as affirmative action, will become progressively less easy to justify if race relations have improved or, more importantly, if significant gains toward equality between African Americans and nonminorities have been made. Valentino and Brader find such an effect for affirmative action—that is, perceptions of improvement in racial discrimination go along with less sup-port for affirmative action. But they do not find this pattern for opposition to welfare, another "racialized" issue that might be similarly linked to perceptions of racial progress.[10]

It makes intuitive sense that people who perceive discrimination to be on the decline would see less need for affirmative action. However, this general argument becomes more strained and improbable when it is suggested that perceptions of decreasing discrimination go hand in hand with *increased* racial resentment and more negative attitudes toward blacks. Valentino and Brader suggest that perceiving less discrimination has the "ironic effect of boosting estimates of racial resentment." They argue further that "the election . . . heightened negative affect toward blacks."[11] They offer the explanation that when levels of perceived discrimination decline, it suggests that *prior* claims of discrimination were unwarranted. Therefore, whites retroactively adjust their current opinions of blacks in a negative direction.

This kind of multi-step thought process is far more involved than what goes into the formation of most opinions. At the same time, this argument is loosely consistent with what has been dubbed the "enlightened racism perspective." Most notably, it has been argued by Sut Jhally and Justin Lewis that atypical black exemplars, such as the Huxtable family on TV's *The Cosby Show* (in which the mother is a lawyer and the father is a doctor), have harmful effects on white attitudes toward blacks because they convince white viewers that anyone can make it and therefore blacks who are not as accomplished as this black family have only themselves to blame.[12]

This version of the theory seems eminently plausible, but to date empirical evidence has been limited to an interpretation of focus group participants who discussed their thoughts and feelings in response to an episode of *The Cosby Show*.[13] Evidence of this kind is obviously open to many possible interpretations, and to date systematic studies have not been able to confirm such an effect. Instead, most empirical evidence suggests precisely the opposite. For example, in three experimental studies that directly tested these competing predictions, Galen Bodenhausen and his colleagues surreptitiously activated specific black exemplars of African American success in order to evaluate their consequences for levels of perceived discrimination against blacks.[14] Did exposure to affluent and highly successful blacks convince whites that discrimination must be on the decline? One experiment found that a successful, positively regarded black exemplar produced *increased* perceptions of discrimination against blacks. A second experiment replicated this finding and also showed that perceptions of successful, but neutrally viewed (rather than liked), blacks did not produce changes in either direction in perceptions of the extent of discrimination that blacks face. A third experiment showed that the effect of well-liked and successful black exemplars in increasing perceptions of discrimination against blacks could be erased if study participants were first reminded that these blacks were atypical. In no case did the exemplars *lower* perceptions of discrimination, as the enlightened racism thesis predicts. Even the fleeting, momentary salience of a successful and likable African American seems to improve whites' intergroup attitudes.

Considering the totality of evidence from past research as well as our own data, we find no reason to believe that the Obama campaign increased white negativity toward blacks. All evidence to date suggests precisely the opposite. In fact, even in Valentino and Brader's own two-wave pre-election panel data, white racial resentment declined significantly during their pre- to post-election panel, although they do not present this particular finding in their article.[15] This positive trend in whites' attitudes toward blacks during the campaign is consistent with our own evidence, shown in chapter 1, as well as with findings from other scholars who found improvement in whites' attitudes toward blacks during the election season.[16]

Although our evidence in chapter 1 corroborates the idea that interracial feelings improved during the election, these aggregate-level data cannot directly determine whether the perceived improvement in race relations goes hand in hand at the individual level with whites harboring more negative attitudes toward blacks, as suggested by Valentino and Brader, or more positive intergroup attitudes, as seems more likely if Obama's strong media presence countered negative black stereotypes. We showed in chapter 1 that white attitudes toward blacks improved during the 2008 campaign year, and in this chapter we show that perceptions of race relations improved during this same period. However, based on these aggregate trends alone, we cannot necessarily conclude that the same whites who perceived improved race relations were not increasing their negative affect toward blacks.

Are these changes over time within individuals related to one another positively, such that positive perceptions of race relations go hand in hand with more positive attitudes toward blacks? Or, as suggested by the enlightened racism thesis, are improvements in perceptions of race relations associated with more negative attitudes toward blacks, even if attitudes on the whole improved? Importantly, although we would not go so far with these data as to assert that one is the cause of the other, it is important to know whether improvement in perceptions of race relations is unquestionably a positive development in how whites view blacks.

In table 3.1, we test this hypothesis using the three-item index of perceptions of race relations as the independent variable, with higher scores indicating improvement. The measure of racial prejudice introduced in chapters 1 and 2, in which higher scores indicate greater prejudice (that is, higher levels of white in-group favoritism), serves as the dependent variable in these analyses. Using a fixed-effects model of within-person change across three waves of

Table 3.1   The Impact of Within-Person Change in Perceptions
of Race Relations on Within-Person Change
in White Racial Prejudice

Wave 3 to 4	−0.91***
	(0.22)
Wave 3 to 5	−1.95***
	(0.22)
Perceptions of race relations	−0.75**
	(0.23)
Constant	9.90***
	(0.37)
Sample size	2,601

Source: 2008 NAES Panel Survey.
Note: The table presents unstandardized fixed-effects coefficients, with standard errors in parentheses. Racial prejudice scores range from 0 to 100, where higher positive values indicate higher levels of prejudice. Perceptions of race relations scores range from −2 to 2, where negative values indicate a pessimistic view, 0 equals a neutral view, and positive values indicate an optimistic view of race relations. The analysis controls for the order in which the racial groups were asked about.
***$p < 0.001$; **$p < 0.01$

panel data, table 3.1 estimates the relationship between change in perceptions of race relations and change in racial prejudice.

In table 3.1, we see that among whites, *improvements* in perceptions of race relations go along with *less* racial prejudice, that is, more positive attitudes toward blacks over time. This is precisely the opposite of what has been suggested by Valentino and Brader. Instead of a post-hoc downgrading of attitudes toward blacks, whites whose perceptions of race relations improved simultaneously became more positive toward blacks. Above and beyond the over-time trend represented by the significant wave coefficients in table 3.1, individuals' improvement in their perceptions of race relations coincided with a decrease in their levels of racial prejudice. The less individuals view race relations as tense, the more equal whites' assessments of blacks and whites become.

Of course, in neither our analysis showing positive effects nor Valentino and Brader's suggesting a negative impact can we rule out potential reverse causation, that is, the possibility that changes in white prejudice toward blacks changed white perceptions of race relations. Nonetheless, what is most important for our purposes is that more positive perceptions of race relations go hand in hand with more positive racial attitudes. We find no evidence of a

Table 3.2   The Impact of Improved and Declining Perceptions of
Race Relations on Change in White Racial Prejudice

	Coeff.	Semirobust Standard Error
Improved perceptions of race relations	−1.40***	0.40
Declining perceptions of race relations	0.09	0.46
Constant	−0.64***	0.16
Sample size	2,601	

Source: 2008 NAES Panel Survey.
Note: The first column presents unstandardized fixed-effects coefficients, with standard errors in the second column. Racial prejudice scores range from 0 to 100, where higher positive values indicate higher levels of prejudice. Perceptions of race relations scores range from −2 to 2, where negative values indicate a pessimistic view, 0 equals a neutral view, and positive values indicate an optimistic view of race relations. The analysis controls for the order in which the racial groups were asked about. A test for the difference between the size of the coefficients for improvement versus decline is statistically significant (chi-square = 5.27; $p = 0.02$).
***$p < 0.001$

double-edged sword in this regard. Perceptions of improvement in race relations do not have the ironic backlash that has been suggested.

One remaining question is whether the ups and downs—the declines and improvements—in perceived race relations are equally tied to racial prejudice. In other words, does the relationship in table 3.1 occur because improvements in perceptions of race relations go along with more egalitarian racial attitudes or because perceived declines in race relations occur when in-group favoritism increases? In table 3.2, we test the symmetry question in the context of a fixed-effects panel analysis. The results make it clear that this relationship is not at all symmetric. Improvements in perceptions of race relations correspond to sizable declines in the extent of prejudice, but the reverse is not true. Declining perceptions of the state of race relations show no relationship whatsoever to over-time increases in levels of white racial prejudice. This asymmetry defies easy explanation, but we suspect that it occurs because the overwhelming direction of change at this point in time is toward more positive perceptions of race relations.

OVERALL IMPLICATIONS OF IMPROVED
PERCEPTIONS OF RACE RELATIONS

In the weeks shortly after the 2008 election, over two-thirds of Americans said that Barack Obama's election as president was either the most important advance for blacks in the last one hundred years or among the two or three most important such advances.[17] The evidence in this chapter confirms that the importance attached to this event by the mass public was not entirely symbolic. Perceptions of race relations improved during the 2008 campaign, particularly among African Americans. Further, this perceived improvement did not cause an increase in negative affect toward blacks. On the contrary, those whose perceptions of race relations became more optimistic also improved in their relative assessment of blacks. Overall, white in-group favoritism declined systematically and significantly during the 2008 campaign.

At the same time, the conventional wisdom about the 2008 election is that it was the most racially polarized, racially divisive election on record.[18] On the surface, this characterization appears to suggest increasingly tense race relations. This story line is in apparent conflict with our evidence that during this same period perceptions of race relations were steadily improving and that white in-group favoritism was declining. Upon closer examination, however, we find that they are quite consistent.

When scholars say that the 2008 election was "racially polarizing," what they mean is not that whites and blacks were out in the streets shouting one another down. Instead, those making this argument are pointing to two kinds of findings that have emerged in post-election research on 2008 voting. First, scholars have noted that race was a stronger predictor of vote choice in 2008 than in previous elections. Notably, it was also the first presidential election with a black candidate representing one of the major political parties. Given that African Americans are much more likely than whites to support Democratic presidential candidates to begin with, what is being noted is that this already strong relationship between race and voting Democratic became even stronger when the Democratic candidate was black. Is it surprising that blacks would be especially likely to support the first black presidential candidate from their favored political party? When viewed in this light, this kind of evidence seems far less threatening and not at all inconsistent with the improved perceptions of race relations that we have described. To call the 2008 election racially "polarizing" is thus somewhat misleading in what it suggests about race relations.

The second type of finding leading to characterizations of racial polarization involves the relationship between racial resentment and candidate preference. What has been dubbed "Obama-induced racialization" refers to the particularly strong relationship between measures of racial resentment and candidate preference in 2008. But again, given that 2008 was the first time a black individual was a major party candidate, it is not surprising that racial resentment played a bigger role in influencing candidate preference and vote choice than it did toward white candidates in the past. How should racial resentment influence a vote choice between two white males to begin with? To gauge whether Americans are more polarized by race than in the past, we would need an electoral contest from the past involving an African American as a major party candidate so we could evaluate whether or not racial resentment was a stronger predictor now than in the past. Lacking such a case for comparison, this claim is less worrisome.

Moreover, the stronger relationship between support for Obama and racial resentment relative to other Democrats is not entirely a sign of antiblack sentiment. As Michael Tesler and David Sears note, "Much of that difference was produced by Obama's strong support from racial liberals."[19] In other words, Obama did not just lose votes from those high on racial resentment; he also gained votes from racial liberals who were *more* likely to vote for him as a result of his race.[20] So to say that candidate preference is racialized is to note simultaneously both positive and negative reactions to race.

To summarize, the 2008 campaign was not a time of increasing racial divisiveness; instead, both whites and blacks, regardless of their political preferences, improved in their relative assessments of one another, and both whites and blacks perceived race relations more generally to have improved. The trends we have outlined should, in and of themselves, be cause for cautious optimism. What should be of greater concern, as will be outlined in part II, is the inherently ephemeral nature of the kinds of effects we observed during Obama's campaign. We address these issues in greater depth in chapter 4 when we describe the theoretical model that best explains these changes and assess the subsequent changes in attitudes that occurred between Obama's election and the end of his first two years in office.

THE BENEFITS OF IMPROVED PERCEPTIONS OF RACE RELATIONS

Even assuming the worst-case scenario that perceptions of race relations are indeed just perceptions, with no connection to the actual incidence of discrimination and no causal relation to decreased prejudice, we think that improved perceptions of race relations are nonetheless generally a positive development. Improved race relations may not signify what we would ideally like, but they may still have a number of worthwhile secondary benefits. These effects are linked to perceived intergroup relations because most people, whites and blacks alike, operate on the basis of day-to-day perceptions, however inaccurate those may be.

As discussed in chapter 2, most white Americans know that overt racism is no longer socially acceptable. As a result, both blacks and whites may suffer from what John Jackson calls "racial paranoia."[21] Both blacks and whites fear conversations about race because they distrust one another and are uncertain what would "count" as racism in the other group's eyes. As a result, Jackson observes, people no longer

> think egalitarian racial language necessarily reflects a speaker's hidden beliefs about race. In a context where getting labeled a racist is "bad for business," most people avoid the theme entirely—at least in mixed company. This dynamic breeds a scenario where, for example, African Americans are skeptical about public expressions of racial inclusion and look for hidden signs of racist hearts ("de cardio racism") beneath race-neutral (even progressive) exteriors.[22]

The intergroup tension inherent in this kind of situation has negative effects on both blacks and whites.

To the extent that people perceive race relations to be improving, one would expect a lessening of these intergroup tensions and a greater willingness to engage. Particularly to the extent that *both* blacks and whites perceive improved race relations, as occurred during the 2008 campaign, one would expect greater trust and prospects for reduced intergroup tension. At the very least, then, improvements in race relations would seem to improve the prospects for communication. As was widely noted in the press, "Mr. Obama does seem to have inspired many to take a step on the road to improved relations—namely, conversation. Cross-racial discussion about the topic of race seems to have become more common, and somewhat less fraught, with the rise of Mr. Obama, according to historians, psychologists, sociologists and other experts on race relations, as well as a number of blacks and whites interviewed around the country."[23]

Feelings of intergroup anxiety among whites and blacks are known to discourage them from interacting.[24] But perhaps more importantly, feelings of intergroup anxiety can make the limited interracial contact that does occur uncomfortable and unproductive. Studies of intergroup contact demonstrate that one of the main reasons intergroup contact often fails to reduce prejudice is the anxiety that people feel in interracial situations. This anxiety ultimately inhibits what would otherwise be beneficial effects of intergroup contact.[25] In other words, anxiety stands in the way of prejudice reduction.

For anyone with doubts about the value of reduced anxiety for improving actual (as opposed to perceived) race relations, the extensive literature on stereotype threat suggests still further reasons why perceptions in and of themselves may have negative consequences. Stereotype threat refers to the fear of confirming a negative stereotype about one's group; ironically, this threat produces a self-fulfilling prophecy in that the heightened awareness of the stereotype leads to more stereotype-confirming behavior. For instance, the fear of confirming the stereotype that blacks are less intelligent than whites contributes to lower academic test scores among blacks than among whites.[26] To the extent that blacks perceive that whites think ill of them in this regard, a key prerequisite for stereotype threat is triggered to undermine black achievement.

Thus far, two studies have examined whether exposure to Obama as a positive role model influenced levels of stereotype threat. One quasi-experimental study by David Marx, Sei Jin Ko, and Ray Friedman revealed better test performance among blacks who participated in the study immediately after Obama's acceptance of the Democratic nomination or immediately after his election relative to test performance among blacks who participated in the study before Obama's acceptance of the nomination or during the fall campaign.[27] These authors theorized that Obama's influence as a salient role model was greatest during times when his counterstereotypical characteristics were most salient. However, a fully randomized lab experiment conducted by Joshua Aronson and his colleagues during the summer of 2008, before the Democratic convention, found no impact of increasing Obama's salience on levels of stereotype threat among black college students.[28] These authors suggest that Obama's success might be seen as unattainable, a perception that would make him ineffectual as a role model. Interestingly, neither study considered the possibility that the campaign itself could have already reduced stereotype threat by altering black perceptions of race relations or the extent of racial stereotyping of blacks by whites. To the extent that Obama made blacks perceive that whites thought better of their group, these perceptions would have had the power to reduce stereotype threat effects.

In addition to greater anxiety and potential stereotype threat effects, studies also suggest that perceptions of poor race relations have negative mental and physical health effects for blacks. Blacks who perceive a great deal of discrimination around them exhibit psychological stress, manifested in such ways as depression and hypertension.[29] Perceived racism also has been found to be associated with many negative psychological and physical health outcomes.[30] Interestingly, a recent meta-analysis of the relationship between perceived racism and poor mental health found a positive association that was moderated by anxiety levels.[31] Overall, findings indicate that perceptions of racism are strongly associated with psychological distress and distrust of others.

To be clear, our point is neither that actual racism is unimportant nor that blacks should delude themselves into thinking that racism has evaporated. But so-called racial optimists, as Obama himself has been dubbed, appear better off in many respects than racial pessimists. For the combination of reasons discussed here, we see it as important to acknowledge improved perceptions of race relations as such and to reap any possible benefits from this change. As we noted early in this chapter, there is no normative consensus as to whether improvement in perceptions of race relations is a positive or negative development. Nonetheless, all available empirical evidence suggests that more positive perceptions of race relations are indeed a good thing for America. Feeling good about race relations—even if the feeling is not accompanied by observable, concrete advances for blacks—goes hand in hand with positive outcomes. It goes along with (1) whites exhibiting more positive attitudes toward blacks (that is, less in-group favoritism); (2) whites becoming less anxious about contact with blacks, and vice versa for blacks; and (3) blacks experiencing less anxiety, threat, and their harmful by-products when they perceive that racial tensions have lessened.

The one documented negative impact of declining perceptions of discrimination is less white support for affirmative action. This presents a dilemma for racial liberals who support affirmative action. Should support for policies designed to redress racial imbalance be the sine qua non of interracial progress? If so, this leads to some perverse admonitions. It suggests that perceiving greater discrimination is the more ideal situation because that perception would increase support for policies designed to reduce racial inequality. Opinions on the effectiveness of affirmative action obviously differ, but even its greatest fans, we think, would happily trade this policy for real reductions in prejudice. On the whole, what happened during the 2008 campaign was a change for the better, not a blow to racial equality, as it has been characterized.[32]

WHOSE PERCEPTIONS CHANGED?

In the remainder of this chapter, we highlight group differences in over-time trends in perceived race relations to better understand their dynamics and implications. We look for evidence illuminating whose perceptions changed the most and then use this as a basis for trying to understand the engines of public perceptions of race discussed in part II. Perceptions are notoriously easy to change relative to reality, and mass media are especially adept at changing mass perceptions in a relatively short period of time. We know that white individuals who moved in the direction of more positive race relations were also somewhat more likely to experience reduced in-group favoritism—that is, less prejudice toward the out-group. So does that imply that perceptions of improved race relations characterize the same groups that declined most in prejudice toward blacks?

Although it would seem logical to assume so, our results suggest that it was not the same people at all. Recall from chapter 2 that, in descriptive terms, it was basically members of the groups who were most prejudiced to begin with who became more egalitarian in their thinking about blacks and whites during the campaign. The people for whom Obama most countered expectations were the ones most influenced by him. Included among those whose levels of racial prejudice declined the most were conservatives, McCain supporters, Republicans, and the less-educated.

In contrast, optimism about race relations under Obama was the province of Obama's natural supporters. Perceptions of race relations moved in an optimistic direction primarily among those one would expect to be excited about Obama's candidacy and election. For example, in figure 3.3, we see that it was Obama supporters who were significantly more likely to shift toward more positive perceptions of race relations. We find the same pattern for Democrats (relative to independents and Republicans) and liberals (compared to moderates and conservatives). The well-educated were also more likely to perceive racial progress during the 2008 campaign, as were younger Americans. In short, the very people who were least prejudiced to begin with were most likely to increase the rosiness of their perceptions of race relations during the 2008 election—precisely the opposite of the groups for whom prejudicial beliefs were most malleable.

This pattern suggests that the change in racial prejudice and the change in perceptions of race relations that both occurred during this period happened for very different reasons. Indeed, the processes underlying these two effects appear to be distinct based on their profiles. The pattern of findings for changed perceptions of race relations makes perfect sense for a process that is thoughtful and information-based: those people who were most likely to be excited about the Obama candidacy and least likely to be prejudiced themselves saw it as cause

Figure 3.3   Change in White Perceptions of Race Relations,
              by Vote Intention

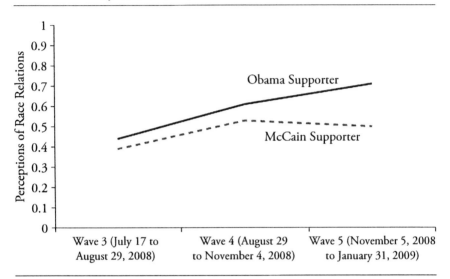

Source: 2008 NAES Panel Survey.
Note: The table presents mean levels of perceptions of race relations separately for whites based on their vote intention on wave 3 (where 0 = support Obama and 1 = support McCain). Only whites who had valid values for the three-item scale measuring perceptions of race relations today, over the last ten years, and over the next ten years on waves 3, 4, and 5 and who indicated that they planned to vote for either Obama or McCain were included (N = 9,510). The scale ranges from −2 to 2, where negative values indicate a pessimistic view, 0 equals a neutral view, and positive values indicate an optimistic view of race relations.

for great optimism about race relations. These people were likely to care a great deal about improvements in race relations and were more invested in and tied to the electoral process. Moreover, a certain amount of wishful thinking was probably also transpiring: more Obama supporters may have wanted to believe in a dramatic positive impact for the country, whereas McCain supporters had no such incentive to project a lessening of racial tensions. Importantly, although racial optimism increased among the citizenry as a whole, these perceptions were particularly likely to improve among those who supported Obama and who were energized by the prospect of a black president and his possible impact on race relations.

Racial prejudice, on the other hand, declined most among those who were least receptive to Obama's message. This makes sense for a process of influence that operates below the radar and outside the realm of mindful awareness. When Americans were inundated with counterstereotypical images of a high-achieving, academically successful, African American family man, their racial attitudes were not influenced by the details of his policy positions. It did not matter that they disagreed with his stance on many, if not all, pressing national issues. He was still an intelligent and successful black man, and that part of his image was never challenged. He might have been portrayed during the campaign as a free-spending socialist, but he was never associated with stereotypically black characterizations of laziness, crime, and broken families. His political coverage was certainly negative at times, but it was a far cry from the usual coverage of African Americans as criminals or welfare recipients.

People are not influenced by the black exemplars they encounter because they consciously think about them and then incorporate them into their over-all judgments of blacks, but rather precisely because they are not conscious of how exemplars inform their views of social groups. For people with negative stereotypes of blacks, Obama was a continual reminder that countered their expectations. As long as the image brought to people's minds when thinking of African Americans was Obama, they were bound to report fewer negative stereotypes than before he came on the national scene.

In part II, we directly link the barrage of media coverage of Obama in 2008 to the changes in prejudice outlined in chapter 1. We examine the surprising role that media exposure to the campaign played in creating the changes we have observed, and we go into greater depth on why these changes affected pre-cisely those people who might be expected to be most impervious to change.

PART II

Explaining Change in White Racial Attitudes During the 2008 Campaign

CHAPTER 4

The Role of Mass Media in Changing White Racial Attitudes

What explains the decline in white racial prejudice that we have observed? Prior public opinion research unfortunately provides little guidance for understanding the processes involved in prejudice reduction. Despite the large amount of research on this general topic, as well as the billions of dollars spent on prejudice reduction efforts in school and work settings, we know shockingly little about effective approaches to this problem. As Elizabeth Paluck and Donald Green note in their review, scholars typically treat "prejudice as a fixed personal attribute," so they rarely consider the causes of *change* in attitudes toward out-groups.[1]

Our theory of mediated intergroup contact suggests that one path to change is mass media exposure to salient out-group exemplars: whether exposure increases or decreases prejudice depends on whether the out-group exemplars confirm or contradict prejudicial stereotypes. In the context of the 2008 presidential campaign, our theory emphasizes the power of the incredible number of images of Obama and his family that firmly refuted stereotypes associating blacks with violence, crime, laziness, and fatherless families. Indeed, one radio host described Obama, "with his wife and two gorgeous daughters," as looking like they were "out of central casting."[2] By contrast, scholars have heavily criticized past media coverage for portraying blacks as criminals and welfare queens, among other negative characterizations.[3] The 2008 campaign clearly shifted the balance of portrayals of blacks in a positive direction, and this may have caused a simultaneous positive shift in racial attitudes.

The foundation for our theory comes from the long line of research on the benefits of *face-to-face* intergroup contact for reducing prejudice. In this case, mass media are hypothesized to play a key role in exposing people to members of out-groups, and particularly in exposing whites to blacks given the limited extent of interracial interaction in daily life. Moreover, media exposure may actually be preferable to face-to-face contact in cases where intergroup anxiety stands in the way of successful interpersonal contact.

Of course, media have long been assumed to play an influential role in intergroup relations, albeit as a cause of conflict rather than harmony. Our theory, by contrast, makes it possible for media to either increase *or* decrease prejudice, depending on the content of out-group portrayals—that is, whether media present mostly positive or mostly negative out-group exemplars. During the 2008 campaign, six months of wall-to-wall coverage of Barack Obama and his family countered racial stereotypes and clearly shifted media portrayals of blacks in a positive direction, thus providing an unprecedented opportunity to examine the effects of mediated intergroup contact.

FACE-TO-FACE INTERGROUP CONTACT

Intergroup contact theory, also known as the "contact hypothesis," proposes that positive interpersonal interactions between members of different social groups can reduce stereotyping and prejudice.[4] This theory has been at the heart of most major efforts to improve intergroup relations over the last century, yet many scholars have long believed that contact works only under highly specific conditions that are rarely met in the real world.[5] As Gordon Allport argued in his 1954 book *The Nature of Prejudice,* contact should work only when in-group and out-group members enjoy (1) equal status in the contact situation, (2) common goals, (3) cooperation, and (4) the support of authorities, law, or custom.

The skepticism of the past has waned in recent years, however, as evidence of contact effects has grown.[6] A recent meta-analysis of 515 studies from 38 countries demonstrated that face-to-face intergroup contact typically reduces stereotyping and prejudice by a modest degree.[7] Moreover, beneficial effects occur even when the contact situation does not meet Allport's critical conditions, though their presence does help to increase the size of the effects.

One explanation for the ease with which contact improves intergroup attitudes is that "mere exposure" helps in-group members feel more comfortable around out-group members.[8] The widely studied "mere exposure" effect suggests that all things being equal, more exposure to a person or object usually improves liking of it.[9] Repeated exposure increases familiarity, and familiarity tends to breed liking.[10] Consistent with this idea, one experimental study found that mere exposure to African American faces increased white participants' liking of other African American faces that they had not seen before.[11]

Mere exposure may partly explain how intergroup contact reduces prejudice, but it still leaves unanswered the question of what constitutes "positive" or "negative" contact. Surely not *all* contact can be expected to reduce prejudice. Unfortunately, while scholars often refer to "positive contact" in their descriptions of intergroup contact theory, most studies provide "virtually no detailed information about the conditions under which the contact occurred," note Thomas Pettigrew and Linda Tropp.[12] We address this issue in the context of media coverage of Obama later in this chapter and also in chapter 5.

Whatever mechanisms are responsible for contact's effects, its potential application on a large scale is reduced if it requires face-to-face interaction. Owing to continued residential segregation, most whites still have limited or superficial interactions with blacks.[13] According to national surveys, few whites report having close friends who are black.[14] Even in the workplace, where self-selection is minimized, many whites say they do not know a black person.[15]

Intergroup anxiety also prevents white and black Americans from interacting more. In some cases, anxiety arises from perceiving the other group as a threat.[16] But even those who have positive feelings about the out-group may feel anxiety because they are unsure about how to interact with out-group members without making "mistakes" that could be interpreted as prejudiced. Intergroup anxiety drives people to avoid future intergroup encounters,[17] and it is also a well-known barrier to achieving benefits even when contact does occur.[18]

MEDIATED INTERGROUP CONTACT

The limitations of face-to-face intergroup contact have led scholars to increasingly emphasize "extended," or "indirect," forms of contact that do not involve direct interpersonal interactions. For instance, research has shown that one need not be friends with an out-group member in order to reap the benefits of contact: simply learning that an in-group friend is friends with an out-group member can lessen prejudice toward the out-group.[19] Along similar lines, observing a friendly interaction between an in-group member and an out-group member can reduce prejudice.[20] In fact, simply *imagining* having a face-to-face interaction with an out-group member can improve attitudes toward the out-group.[21]

Mass media exposure to out-group members represents an especially prom-ising form of indirect contact. Most people are more likely to be exposed to out-group members via mass media than through face-to-face contact. Given the omnipresence of mass media in contemporary life, mass media have the potential to act as a key point of "contact" between in-group and out-group members, especially blacks and whites. In light of the beneficial effects from "mere exposure" to out-group members, the sheer amount of exposure to out-group members via mass media may help to increase in-group members' familiarity and comfort with the out-group, thus reducing prejudice.[22]

Mass media could be particularly advantageous because they provide oppor-tunities for "contact" without the anxiety that often characterizes face-to-face intergroup interactions. In-group members are presumably less likely to avoid portrayals of out-groups on television than in face-to-face encounters, yet both contexts provide opportunities for exposure to the out-group. Exposure to out-group portrayals via mass media ought to involve less anxiety than face-to-face interactions. At the same time, viewers must still accept media portrayals of out-group members as informative about the real-world out-group. Consistent with this possibility, research on human-media interaction suggests that viewers psychologically process mediated information—especially social content—as if it came from firsthand observation. Because the brain has not evolved a special mechanism to distinguish between mediated and unmediated content, people automatically and unconsciously react to people on television in fundamentally the same ways as they do to real people and events.[23]

To be sure, people do not run out of the room to call 911 when they see a fire on television, but they do exhibit many of the same psychological reactions (such as fear) and physiological reactions (such as arousal), albeit with less intensity than if a fire had actually broken out in their own living room. So, for example, exposure to a human being who appears larger and closer owing to a larger television screen produces more generalized arousal and attention than exposure to the same content on a smaller screen.[24] The same reactions occur when one is approached by another person in real life: as the other person comes closer, he or she appears larger by taking up a greater portion of one's field of vision.

The theoretical basis for expecting mediated contact with out-group mem-bers to influence stereotyping and prejudice is strong. In contrast, empirical evidence of such effects is surprisingly thin.[25] The vast majority of studies rely on cross-sectional surveys that at best demonstrate significant relationships between exposure to out-group members and higher or lower levels of prejudice.[26] However, these cross-sectional correlations provide a weak basis for causal claims. Failure to control for variables that are related to both exposure and prejudice may produce spurious associations.[27] Moreover, reverse causation may account for the association between exposure and prejudice. People may selectively expose themselves to media content that is congruent with their preexisting prejudices, especially when such media content wears its out-group politics on its sleeve.[28]

Nonetheless, several laboratory experiments have convincingly demonstrated that media exposure can in fact alter levels of prejudice.[29] In one study, participants viewed a television comedy skit that portrayed blacks either stereotypically (poor, uneducated, and violent) or not stereotypically.[30] Those who viewed the nonstereotypical skit were less likely to believe that a black suspect in an unrelated situation was guilty of physical assault. In another study, participants read a newsletter about a black college student that either reinforced or countered negative racial stereotypes.[31] Those who read the counterstereotypical newsletter were less likely to endorse antiblack stereotypes or to generalize those stereotypes to unrelated situations.

These experimental studies clearly demonstrate that media exposure has *the potential* to change attitudes toward out-groups, but what remains to be seen is whether these findings generalize to more naturalistic settings, such as the rough-and-tumble of a presidential campaign. For the most part, real-world effects of mediated contact have simply been assumed without documentation. These assertions notably lack evidence that individuals change their attitudes and that they do so in response to media exposure. Our study, in contrast, uses panel data to directly link mediated exposure to Obama with changes in racial attitudes at the individual level.

OUT-GROUP EXEMPLARS AND MASS MEDIA

We expect exposure to mass media to influence levels of prejudice primarily through exposure to highly salient out-group exemplars. "Exemplification" refers to the idea that attitudes toward social groups are based in large part on the exemplars who most readily come to mind.[32] Thus, drawing attention to individual out-group members alters attitudes toward the out-group as a whole. For example, drawing attention to politicians embroiled in scandal reduces trust in politicians as a group,[33] while drawing attention to a well-respected politician produces more favorable attitudes toward his or her political party.[34]

Along these same lines, several laboratory experiments have demonstrated that *recent* and *short-term* exposure to African American exemplars influences attitudes toward blacks as a group. Of particular importance for our study, exposure to well-liked and counterstereotypical black exemplars has been shown to reduce prejudice toward blacks. One experiment found that surreptitious exposure to Oprah Winfrey or Michael Jordan promoted more sympathetic attitudes toward blacks.[35] Another experiment produced similar results from brief exposure to positive black exemplars such as Martin Luther King Jr., Colin Powell, and Bill Cosby.[36]

Further research has manipulated characteristics of the same African American exemplars in order to highlight the differential impact of reinforcing versus countering negative racial stereotypes. White participants in one experiment viewed photos of the same black individual's face set against the background of either the interior of a church or a street corner with a graffiti-covered wall.[37] Those who viewed the picture with the graffiti-covered wall expressed more antiblack bias than those who viewed the picture with the interior of a church. Similar results have been found by varying the background between a church and a prison and, within the prison context, by varying a black man's clothing to make him look like a lawyer (wearing a formal suit) or a prisoner (wearing an orange jumpsuit).[38]

In sum, exemplification effects are a well-established phenomenon, with numerous experimental studies providing strong causal evidence that highly visible exemplars of social groups can change attitudes toward the group they exemplify. Brief exposure to images of black exemplars in particular has been shown to either increase or decrease racial prejudice depending on whether the images reinforce or refute negative racial stereotypes.

Can mass media exposure to out-group exemplars similarly influence attitudes toward out-groups? Many studies of "exemplification in communication" have demonstrated that mediated exposure to exemplars influences a range of perceptions and attitudes, though much less evidence pertains to out-group exemplars and prejudice specifically.[39] Nonetheless, the theoretical framework offered by exemplification, as well as by "cultivation" and the "parasocial contact" hypothesis, suggests that media exposure to out-group exemplars can influence levels of stereotyping and prejudice.[40] What remains to be seen is whether mediated exposure to out-group exemplars can influence levels of prejudice in a real-world context such as an election campaign. To observe such an effect requires a naturally occurring context in which the usual flow of exemplars corresponding to an out-group is fundamentally altered within the period of the study.

The 2008 campaign provides a particularly difficult test of whether media exposure to counterstereotypical out-group exemplars can reduce prejudice in a naturalistic setting. To date, research has been inconclusive about whether racial prejudice declined during the 2008 campaign and, if it did, what impact exposure to the Obama exemplar had. A small-scale laboratory experiment conducted long after the 2008 campaign using a college student sample found that exposure to Obama reduced white racial prejudice.[41] But it is unknown whether naturally occurring exposure during the campaign had a similar impact. As described in chapter 1, Susan Welch and Lee Sigelman relied on cross-sectional surveys executed by the American National Election Studies to show a positive *aggregate* shift in whites' attitudes toward blacks from 2004 to 2008, after little change in attitudes had occurred during the preceding decade.[42] Because these data were collected only at four-year intervals, however, they leave open many alternative explanations.[43] Moreover, no studies to date have linked changes in racial prejudice to exposure to Obama.

Overall, prior research suggests that an "Obama effect" leading to reductions in white racial prejudice is plausible, although there is no direct evidence linking exposure to Obama to declines in prejudice. Chapters 1 and 2 documented a significant decline in racial prejudice during the 2008 campaign. This decline was particularly pronounced among whites with higher initial levels of racial prejudice, including McCain supporters, Republicans, and conservatives. Next we use three waves of panel data to test the hypothesis that mass public exposure to the Obama exemplar helped to produce these reductions in racial prejudice.

MEASURING EXPOSURE TO THE OBAMA EXEMPLAR

The innumerable images of Obama and his family during the 2008 campaign clearly contradicted prevailing stereotypes of African Americans, but did ongoing exposure to these images translate into more positive attitudes toward African Americans as a whole? To answer this question we relied on three waves of nationally representative panel data and multiple measures of exposure to Obama.

How were people exposed to the Obama exemplar? Although few individuals saw Obama in person at rallies, millions of Americans saw Obama on television. We focus on television because it is by far the most widely used media source, and also because it most closely approximates the audiovisual characteristics of face-to-face intergroup contact. We employ three measures of televised exposure to the Obama exemplar: change in the number of political TV shows viewed, change in general political interest, and change in self-perceived knowledge about Obama.

To assess the number of television programs respondents viewed that were likely to include coverage of Obama, our measure included a broad range of genres, such as hard news programs (*ABC World News Tonight*), soft news programs (*60 Minutes*), opinion programs (*The O'Reilly Factor*), political talk shows (*This Week with George Stephanopoulos*), mostly nonpolitical talk shows (*Oprah*), and satirical programs (*The Daily Show*).[44] Because many programs beyond traditional network news cover political campaigns today, our measure tapped regular viewership of the forty-nine most-watched programs based on Nielsen ratings that included any campaign-related content.[45]

The number of political TV shows viewed is a highly reliable measure of political television exposure.[46] Moreover, it has been demonstrated to predict the sorts of things that exposure to political television ought to predict, including gains in knowledge about campaign issues as the presidential campaign unfolds. In sum, this measurement is both reliable and has strong predictive validity, as indicated by the fact that individual changes over time in exposure predict gains in knowledge about candidates.

To ensure that our findings do not rest on any one particular measurement strategy, we also tapped exposure to the Obama exemplar with two additional measures. One is a measure of general political interest, a common approach to assessing campaign exposure.[47] Respondents were asked at three points in time how interested they were in politics and public affairs. Although political interest is obviously confounded with many other individual characteristics in a cross-sectional survey, our panel analyses focus strictly on within-person change in political interest over time. What is important for our purposes is the idea that increases over time in political interest should go hand in hand with increases in campaign exposure.

Our third measure tapped exposure to Obama specifically. At three points in time, respondents were asked how well they felt they knew Obama, that is, they were asked about their self-perceived knowledge about Obama. Although such perceptions are undoubtedly subjective, fluctuations over time in an individual's self-perceived knowledge should track fluctuations in campaign exposure, with increases over time in exposure presumably leading to concomitant increases in his or her self-perceived knowledge about candidates. We scale this measure, along with our other exposure variables, to range from 0 to 1. Racial prejudice ranges from 0 to 100, though nearly all respondents had values in the range of 0 to 35.

To examine the effects of exposure to the Obama exemplar, we gauge the impact of changes over time in exposure on changes over time in prejudice *at the individual level.* A fixed-effects panel analysis tells us whether the individuals whose exposure to Obama increased were the same individuals whose racial prejudice decreased over time (and vice versa).[48] This analysis is unlike most observational studies, and even most panel analyses, which incorporate cross-sectional variance and thus compare different people to one another. The most common observational study employs a cross-sectional survey to assess the association between exposure and prejudice. Between-person analyses are widely acknowledged to provide weak causal evidence. By contrast, fixed-effects panel analyses look only at change *within the same person* from one point in time to another. This is different from lagged dependent variable approaches to panel analysis, which utilize both over-time and between-person variance. Using fixed effects, individual differences such as education, income, gender, age, party affiliation, political ideology, and ongoing political interest drop out of the equation, as do all unmeasured variables that do not change. Characteristics that remain stable over time obviously cannot predict change. Using this approach, we are able to take into account the average change that occurred across all respondents by including dummy variables representing wave, while simultaneously eliminating the potential for confounding based on stable individual differences.[49] As a result, fixed-effects regression arguably provides the strongest causal evidence outside of randomized experiments.[50]

At the same time, fixed-effects regression does have one weakness: it provides extremely conservative estimates of effects. Other panel analyses, such as lagged dependent variable approaches, "use information both within and between individuals," notes Paul Allison. "Fixed effects estimates, on the other hand, use only within-individual differences, essentially discarding any information about differences between individuals."[51] Thus, by using fixed-effects regression, we produce conservative estimates of media effects that are not confounded with stable individual differences.[52]

THE IMPACT OF EXPOSURE TO OBAMA ON RACIAL PREJUDICE

Table 4.1 presents fixed-effects models of within-person change, with each column presenting a separate statistical model predicting change in racial prejudice from change in each of the three measures of exposure to Obama. The

Table 4.1   The Effects of Within-Person Change in Exposure
to Obama on Within-Person Change
in White Racial Prejudice

	(1)	(2)	(3)
Time			
Wave 3 to 4	−.84**	−0.64*	−.77**
	(0.25)	(0.27)	(0.27)
Wave 3 to 5	−1.96***	−1.81***	−1.76***
	(0.25)	(0.27)	(0.27)
Exposure to Obama			
Number of political	−4.51*		
TV shows viewed	(1.88)		
Political interest		−2.91**	
		(0.90)	
Self-perceived knowledge			−1.46*
about Obama			(0.71)
Constant	10.61***	12.81***	11.12***
	(0.53)	(1.01)	(0.78)
Sample size	2,065	1,812	1,804

Source: 2008 NAES Panel Survey.
Note: The table presents unstandardized fixed-effects regression coefficients with standard errors in parentheses. All of the independent variables range from 0 to 1. Each model also includes the order in which the racial groups were asked about.
***$p < 0.001$; **$p < 0.01$; *$p < 0.05$; all two-tailed

first column reveals a significant impact of change over time in the number of political TV shows viewed on change in racial prejudice. Because we recoded our variable for political television viewing to range from 0 to 1, and racial prejudice ranges from 0 to 100, the coefficient of −4.51 for political television viewing suggests that whites whose exposure to Obama during the campaign increased the most showed average reductions in racial prejudice of four and a half points between each pair of survey waves. Across all three waves, this translates into a nine-point decline in racial prejudice due to exposure to Obama over the course of the campaign.

This is a relatively large effect. Recall from chapter 2 that the overall decline in racial prejudice was just two points; even this was big by historical standards given how little prejudice usually changes in a six-month time period. But among those with the greatest amount of exposure to Obama, the decline in prejudice was more than four times greater. Thus, by assessing individual exposure to Obama, we obtain not only stronger causal evidence of the Obama effect but also evidence of a larger effect size.

Using our two other measures of exposure to Obama, we also find significant evidence of impact, though these weaker measures understandably produce smaller estimates of the size of the effects. The model in column 2 of table 4.1 shows that increases over time in political interest produced reductions in racial prejudice of about three points between each pair of waves, or six points across all three waves. Following the same pattern, the model in column 3 reveals a significant impact of changes in self-perceived knowledge about Obama, with increases over time in knowledge producing reductions in racial prejudice of about one and a half points between each pair of waves, or three points across all three waves.

Again, these analyses strictly compare individuals to themselves at an earlier point in time, so differences between individuals drop out of the equations. Because our models predict change over time in racial prejudice, only factors that also change over time can affect the results.[53]

To be sure, media exposure to Obama was not the only thing that changed during the campaign, though it does provide the most obvious explanation for the unusually large decline in racial prejudice relative to the previous twenty years. For example, an alternative explanation might lie in the economic collapse that began in 2007, though a deterioration in economic conditions should, if anything, increase prejudice, owing to heightened economic competition with the out-group over jobs and other material resources.[54] In any case, our own analyses show that individuals' perceptions of their family finances and national economic conditions had no effect on changes in racial prejudice and so left our estimates of the impact of media exposure unchanged.

The top two rows of table 4.1 show that racial prejudice also declined between each pair of waves for reasons having nothing to do with the campaign. We are not aware of any other major national events that occurred during the fall of 2008 that could explain the decline in racial prejudice. Nonetheless, we controlled for the average sum-total effects of all else that changed during the campaign by including the wave variables in the analyses. Thus, to the extent that political interest or some other factor increased across the board during the campaign, the wave variables capture those influences.[55] The wave variables also capture any impact of a long-term secular trend in prejudice that preceded and then continued through the campaign.

THE ADDITIONAL IMPACT OF CAMPAIGN ADVERTISING

Across three different measures of exposure, we find consistent evidence that exposure to Obama led to reductions in white racial prejudice. Because all three measures can be criticized for relying on respondents' self-reports, we conducted an additional test using data on variation between states in the amount of television advertising by the Obama campaign. Although nationally all TV viewers were exposed to Obama through television programs, whites living in states with more political advertising should have experienced additional exposure to Obama and thus have had larger reductions in racial prejudice.

Although detailed data on television advertising spending by media markets are prohibitively expensive, estimates of advertising spending by state are publicly available.[56] For our purposes, we have categorized states into the top twenty-five and the bottom twenty-five in Obama advertising spending, though we find similar results using alternative categorizations.[57]

Figure 4.1 presents levels of racial prejudice by amount of television advertising spending by the Obama campaign. Because campaign advertising had concluded by election day, the figure shows the trend in prejudice from wave 3 (the summer of 2008) through wave 4 (the fall of 2008), excluding the post-election wave. As shown in figure 4.1, racial prejudice declined to a greater extent among whites living in states where there was more advertising by the Obama campaign. A fixed-effects model confirms that the extent of decline over time in prejudice was significantly greater in high-advertising states. Whites living in states with less exposure to Obama stayed roughly flat in their levels of prejudice, whereas the prejudice levels of those in states with high levels of Obama exposure declined more steeply. A negative and significant interaction between the wave 3 to 4 dummy variable and a dummy variable indicating residence in one of the top twenty-five states confirms the statistical significance of this finding (-1.04, $p < 0.05$, N = 2,627).

The state-by-state differences in Obama advertising spending also provide an opportunity for another test of our theory. Campaign advertising often appears during the commercial breaks of political television programs, a natural opportunity to expose potential voters. As a result, the impact of viewing political television programs should also be larger in states with more campaign advertising because respondents would have been exposed to Obama

Figure 4.1   Change in White Racial Prejudice in the Top Twenty-Five and the Bottom Twenty-Five States in Television Advertising Spending by the Obama Campaign

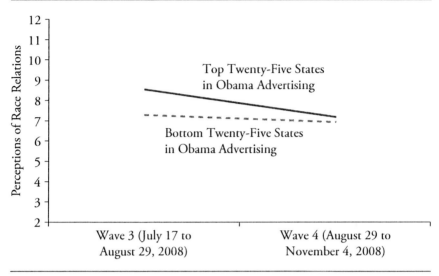

Source: 2008 NAES Panel Survey.

Note: To confirm that racial prejudice declined more among whites living in the top twenty-five states in television advertising spending by the Obama campaign, we conducted a fixed-effects regression analysis predicting within-person change in white racial prejudice from the wave 4 dummy variable (with wave 3 as the excluded reference category) and its interaction with a dummy variable where 1 equals living in one of the top twenty-five states in Obama advertising and 0 equals living in one of the bottom twenty-five states in Obama advertising. The analysis shows a negative and significant interaction (-1.04, $p < 0.05$, N = 2,627).

both through the programs and through the advertising appearing during the commercial breaks. Consistent with this hypothesis, increases over time in the number of political TV shows viewed produced larger reductions in racial prejudice among whites living in the top twenty-five states in Obama advertising. That is, a fixed-effects model reveals a negative and significant interaction between change in the number of political TV shows viewed and residence in one of the top twenty-five states (-11.49, $p = 0.06$, N = 2,060). Both of these findings based on completely different sources of exogenous variance in Obama exposure point to the same conclusion about the importance of exposure to a counterstereotypical exemplar.

CONSERVATIVES AND THE OBAMA EFFECT

In chapter 2, we found larger declines in racial prejudice among McCain voters, conservatives, and Republicans. If our general theory is correct, this should have occurred because these groups were more affected than liberals and Democrats by the coverage of Obama. To address this question we examined whether the impact of exposure to Obama on prejudice was larger among McCain supporters than among Obama supporters.

We tested this proposition using interactions between the exposure variables— that is, change over time in the number of political TV shows viewed, political interest, and self-perceived knowledge about Obama—and vote intention in fixed-effects models. Although the main effects of individual differences, including vote intention, drop out of fixed-effects models, it is still possible to include interactions between individual differences and variables that do change over time. To test the hypothesis that increases over time in exposure to Obama produce larger declines in racial prejudice among McCain supporters than among Obama supporters, we ran a model including an interaction between vote intention and exposure.

Table 4.2 presents our results, with each column showing a different fixed-effects model that interacts vote intention with one of the three exposure variables. Because vote intention is coded so that 0 represents Obama supporters and 1 represents McCain supporters, a negative interaction indicates that exposure to Obama produced larger reductions in racial prejudice among McCain supporters than among Obama supporters. As shown in table 4.2, all of the interactions are negative (and two are statistically significant), which is consistent with a larger Obama effect among McCain supporters than among Obama supporters. We also find the same results using political ideology or party affiliation in place of vote intention.

These findings may seem counterintuitive to many political scientists, but they are consistent with the unique psychological process underlying mediated intergroup contact. According to the theory, what matters for attitudes toward out-groups is which out-group exemplars happen to be at the "top of mind." Exemplification thus operates without deliberative processing, and this minimizes resistance to counterstereotypical portrayals. As one experiment found, only when people are forewarned *not* to be influenced by atypical exemplars does exposure to highly successful black exemplars like Michael Jordan or Oprah Winfrey fail to improve attitudes toward blacks.[58] So while Republicans and

Table 4.2   The Effects of Within-Person Change in Exposure to
Obama on Within-Person Change in White Racial
Prejudice, by Vote Intention

	(1)	(2)	(3)
Time			
Wave 3 to 4	−0.87**	−0.68*	−0.83**
	(0.28)	(0.30)	(0.29)
Wave 3 to 5	−1.96***	−1.80***	−1.76***
	(0.28)	(0.30)	(0.30)
Exposure to Obama			
Number of political	−0.15		
TV shows viewed	(3.24)		
Political interest		0.17	
		(1.62)	
Self-perceived knowledge			−1.19
about Obama			(1.33)
Vote Intention × Exposure			
McCain Supporter × TV	−9.34*		
	(4.21)		
McCain Supporter × Interest		−5.28*	
		(2.11)	
McCain Supporter ×			−0.84
Knowledge about Obama			(1.65)
Constant	10.97***	12.22***	11.14***
	(0.59)	(0.88)	(0.69)
Sample size	1,714	1,495	1,489

Source: 2008 NAES Panel Survey.
Note: The table presents unstandardized fixed-effects regression coefficients, with standard errors in parentheses. Vote intention was measured on wave 3 (0 equals support for Obama and 1 equals support for McCain). Each model also includes the order in which the racial groups were asked about. Note that the main effects of vote intention drop out of fixed-effects models of within-person change because it is a constant and thus does not change over time.
***$p < 0.001$; **$p < 0.01$; *$p < 0.05$; all two-tailed

conservatives undoubtedly resisted Obama's political message, the images of Obama still refuted negative racial stereotypes *implicitly.*

The passive psychological process underlying exemplification explains why exposure to Obama influenced the racial views of conservatives, but why was the effect *larger* among conservatives than among liberals? Again, this may seem counterintuitive, but it is consistent with how mediated contact should work. Research on "extremity bias" finds that people are more influenced by extreme or novel information that strongly contrasts with their expectations.[59] Consistent with these studies, intergroup contact causes the largest reductions in prejudice among those for whom the out-group exemplar most strongly counters their expectations of the out-group—that is, those with higher initial levels of prejudice.[60] Because Republicans and conservatives have higher initial levels of racial prejudice, Obama countered their expectations about blacks far more than he did for people with more positive expectations.

DID THE POLITICAL SLANT OF COVERAGE MATTER?

Individuals obviously did not need to support Obama in order for their prejudice levels to decline, but did the partisanship of the media coverage of Obama also condition the extent of reductions in racial prejudice? Given the frequent tirades against the opposition featured on partisan television programs, it seems natural to wonder whether such strident coverage could possibly decrease prejudice.

At least according to the theory, the political tone of the coverage of Obama should not have mattered so long as it portrayed Obama in ways that countered negative racial stereotypes. Based on our observations across the media spectrum, criticism of Obama was not generally aimed at traditional racial stereotypes such as laziness, untrustworthiness, or lack of intelligence. Even conservative programs that harshly criticized Obama's politics nonetheless portrayed him as hardworking rather than lazy, as well educated and intelligent, and as a trusted family man rather than a violent criminal. Thus, even exposure to Obama through conservative programs should theoretically have produced declines in racial prejudice.

To test this hypothesis we examine whether the partisan slant of programs mattered above and beyond the sheer number of political television programs viewed. We relied on prior research categorizing television programs as leaning toward Democrats, as learning toward Republicans, or as generally neutral.[61] We then divided the number of conservative, liberal, and neutral programs by the total number of political TV shows viewed, producing three variables for each wave of measurement: proportion conservative, proportion liberal, and proportion neutral.

Table 4.3   The Effects of Within-Person Change in Partisan
             Media Exposure on Within-Person Change in
             White Racial Prejudice

Wave 3 to 4	−0.80**
	(0.25)
Wave 3 to 5	−1.94***
	(0.25)
Number of political TV shows viewed	−3.36#
	(1.98)
Proportion conservative	−2.05*
	(0.89)
Proportion liberal	−0.78
	(0.88)
Proportion neutral	−0.75
	(0.74)
Constant	11.19***
	(0.62)
Sample size	2,065

Source: 2008 NAES Panel Survey.
Note: The table presents unstandardized fixed-effects regression coefficients, with standard errors in parentheses. All of the independent variables range from 0 to 1. Each model also includes the order in which the racial groups were asked about.
***$p < 0.001$; **$p < 0.01$; *$p < 0.05$; #$p < 0.10$; all two-tailed

As shown in table 4.3, our analyses revealed that racial prejudice declined even as a function of viewing partisan programs that were critical of Obama. In fact, the fixed-effects model shows that increases over time in the proportion conservative produced significant declines in racial prejudice, even after controlling for changes in the overall number of programs viewed. Put another way, regardless of how many programs one viewed—that is, the overall amount of exposure to Obama—the extent to which that exposure occurred via conservative programs produced some additional reductions in racial prejudice. This makes sense in light of the fact that more conservatives than liberals watch conservative programs. These findings support our theoretical prediction that exposure to Obama should reduce prejudice because of coverage portraying him as countering negative racial stereotypes, even if that coverage was critical of him politically.

These findings also imply support for the direction of our causal argument that changes over time in exposure to Obama led to declines in prejudice rather than the reverse causal order. Whites who disliked Obama and had higher levels of preexisting prejudice were likely to avoid exposure to Obama, resulting in no change in racial prejudice. But here we find that racial prejudice declined the most among whites who viewed conservative television programs and had *higher* levels of preexisting racial prejudice, including McCain supporters, conservatives, and Republicans. Other than reverse causation, the only other threat to a causal interpretation would be if some other third force produced both declines in prejudice and increases in exposure. We cannot think of any such force beyond those already ruled out earlier in this chapter.

Taken together, this evidence strongly supports our hypothesis that media exposure to Obama during the 2008 campaign helped to reduce white racial prejudice. Despite the strengths and weaknesses corresponding to the three exposure measures, increases over time in exposure to Obama led to declines in racial prejudice at the individual level. Moreover, although exposure occurred primarily through national television programs, additional exposure in states with an influx of television advertising by Obama led to further reductions in racial prejudice.

Consistent with our theory of mediated intergroup contact, these effects were not driven by Obama's political supporters. On the contrary, exposure to Obama produced the largest reductions in prejudice among McCain supporters, conservatives, and Republicans. This may seem counterintuitive to scholars who primarily study overtly persuasive appeals, but it makes a great deal of sense in the context of exposure to positive black exemplars. The portrayals of Obama countering negative racial stereotypes were not overtly persuasive campaign messages, and they may even have been quite critical of Obama's policies. As a result, these implicit messages about blacks bypassed the sort of conscious deliberation and resistance that has been found in response to overtly antiracist messages.[62] Instead, exemplification influenced attitudes toward out-groups through a passive psychological process. Exposure to Obama influenced those with higher initial prejudice the most because he countered their expectations of blacks far more than he did among those with more positive expectations.

These findings are very encouraging for efforts to improve intergroup relations through mediated intergroup contact. The beneficial effects from exposure to Obama clearly contradict subtyping theory, which predicts that whites would have dismissed Obama as an exception to prevailing racial stereotypes.[63] Subtyping suggests that although intergroup contact may improve attitudes toward those individual out-group members with whom in-group members have interactions, these effects are unlikely to be generalized to the out-group as a whole.[64] Allport called this problem "re-fencing": "There are nice negroes but . . . or some of my best friends are Jews but . . . by excluding a few favored cases, the negative rubric is kept intact for all other cases."[65]

For decades, subtyping provided the impetus for skepticism that intergroup contact could effectively reduce prejudice. In stark contrast to the pessimism of subtyping theory, a recent meta-analysis showed that intergroup contact usually improves attitudes toward out-groups, especially among those with more negative preexisting images of the out-group.[66] In recent years, a growing body of evidence has also shown that exposure to counterstereotypical exemplars can reduce stereotyping and prejudice.[67] Even exposure to highly atypical exemplars—those who should be most likely to be dismissed as exceptions—can reduce prejudice.

Mediated intergroup contact may be especially likely to subvert potential subtyping because the portrayals of out-group members are typically incidental to the plots of most television programs, whether fictional or nonfiction. Ironically, the exceptions are those programs that are designed to reduce prejudice but often fail to do so.[68] Most programs do not wear their out-group politics on their sleeves, thus minimizing the extent to which viewers consciously process and resist the portrayals based on their preexisting prejudices. Indeed, the classic example of a program failing to reduce prejudice as intended is the iconic 1970s sitcom *All in the Family,* which included a great deal of content designed to smack viewers upside the head with the message that racism is bad. The problem with this blatant strategy was that it made it easy for racially prejudiced viewers to either miss the intended humor or identify the message as contrary to their views, reject its premise, and subsequently hold on to their antiblack attitudes.[69] Media coverage of the 2008 Obama campaign, by contrast, exposed millions of white Americans to a counterstereotypical black exemplar much more surreptitiously.

CHAPTER 5

Testing Rival Theories of Media Influence

Mass public exposure to the 2008 presidential campaign played an important role in helping to reduce whites' racial prejudice during the fall of 2008. We have hypothesized that this decline in prejudice resulted from media exposure to Barack Obama as a positive black exemplar. According to exemplification theory, attitudes about social groups are based on the individual group members, or exemplars, who most readily come to mind. So when asked for their attitudes about blacks, whites' responses are based on the individual African Americans who are most readily accessible in their minds. This theory predicts that the sheer amount of coverage of Obama, who so clearly and strongly countered negative racial stereotypes, made him the most salient black exemplar in the minds of whites, resulting in a positive shift in whites' views of blacks as a group.

Exemplification provides an intuitive and elegant explanation for the 2008 campaign's impact on racial prejudice. The most notable element of the campaign was the massive amount of coverage of Obama countering racial stereotypes, which clearly and decisively shifted the flow of black exemplars in mass media in a positive direction. Researchers have studied media portrayals of blacks for decades, and with rare exception they have concluded that mass media portray blacks primarily in a negative light, associating them with violent crime, laziness, and fatherless families. The 2008 campaign, through wall-to-wall coverage of Obama and his family, made the prototypical image of blacks on television a positive one, at least temporarily.

Although exemplification is a highly plausible explanation for the campaign's impact on racial prejudice, some alternatives remain, so in this chapter we address three plausible rival theories. Whereas exemplification emphasizes the sheer amount of coverage of Obama, the three alternative theories point to different aspects of that coverage, such as whether campaign coverage highlighted ongoing racism in society or actively promoted racial unity between whites and blacks. Either of these types of coverage could have had a positive impact on racial attitudes.

In the next section, we look at three types of coverage and the theories of influence underlying them as potential rival explanations. Then we proceed to empirical tests of the impact of exposure to each type of coverage on racial attitudes during the campaign. For this purpose, we rely on a large-scale content analysis of campaign coverage combined with our best measure of individuals' media exposure to the campaign. Using our panel data, we are able to assess whether changes over time in exposure to each type of coverage produced changes over time in racial prejudice at the individual level.

COVERAGE HIGHLIGHTING RACISM

One alternative to the mediated intergroup contact explanation is that Obama campaign coverage reduced white racial prejudice by focusing national attention on the continuing presence of racism in American society. News throughout the campaign included stories about whites who said that they would not vote for Obama because he is black. Stereotype suppression theory suggests that this type of coverage induced whites to feel self-conscious about their racial attitudes and thus led them to reevaluate and ultimately change their views about blacks.[1]

Stories about racism during the campaign focused most often on the impact of white racial prejudice on vote choice. As the headline of one CNN story proclaimed, "Race Could Play a Big Role in Election." The story relayed survey findings suggesting that racism could cost Obama about six percentage points of the final tally, which turned out to be very close to the estimates produced by researchers after the election. Other news stories went further, suggesting that the effects of overt racism would be overshadowed by even larger effects of "unconscious racism." The *Seattle Post-Intelligencer* reported that although some whites were "dyed-in-the-wool racists," many more "discriminate unconsciously" but "don't think they're racist."[2] As it turned out, post-election studies demonstrated that unconscious racism did not influence vote choice above and beyond levels of overt racism.[3] Nonetheless, coverage of racism seems particularly capable of prompting whites to feel self-conscious about their own, possibly hidden, racial biases.

Even after the election, news coverage examined the continuing impact of racism. As one headline asked, "Why Is Obama Our First Black President?" The implicit question here was, why has there not been a black president until now?[4] Another story, in answer, concluded that "prejudices are very, very virulent and deeply ingrained." In fact, despite many claims that the news media bought into the notion of a postracial America and ignored the effects of ongoing racism, many stories acknowledged both the obvious progress that had been made and the problems that remained. As one headline read, "Road to Racial Tolerance Is Paved, but Potholes Persist."[5] Moreover, other stories covered the backlash among racist whites who were extremely angry about Obama's election, including cross-burnings, assassination threats, and vandalism with racial slurs.[6] Of course, race-based vandalism occurred during the campaign as well, but the Obama campaign downplayed such incidents out of concern that any attention drawn to race would hurt Obama at the polls.[7]

Experimental evidence from stereotype suppression theory suggests that exposure to campaign coverage that explicitly discussed white racism could have helped spur reductions in racial prejudice. For instance, one study found that informing whites that their responses in a survey exhibit racial bias leads to lower levels of prejudice on later, purportedly unrelated tasks.[8] In another study, instructing whites to avoid racial prejudice also led to lower levels of prejudice on later tasks.[9] One might reasonably wonder if such findings are confounded by experimenter demand—that is, by the study participants' awareness that the research investigator wants certain answers. The use of behavior on later tasks that participants believe to be part of different studies, however, should reduce experimenter demand.

Perhaps more convincing, other experimental studies have avoided directly communicating an antiracist message to participants, instead letting the message be communicated by subtle means. For example, merely observing others express antiracist views can lead to reductions in racial prejudice. In each of several experiments, seeing a white confederate's antiracist responses on a questionnaire reduced prejudice, compared to those without any knowledge of the confederate's responses. Importantly, participants were led to believe that they were viewing the confederate's responses without the confederate's knowledge.[10]

The psychological mechanism that is assumed to underlie these effects is self-reflection. Consistent with this expectation, a series of experiments have manipulated levels of "self-focus" and thus reduced levels of prejudice, even though the manipulations made no mention of prejudice.[11] Those assigned to the high-self-focus conditions completed surveys while they sat in front of mirrors or television monitors with their faces shown on them, while those assigned to the low-self-focus conditions completed the surveys without the mirrors or television monitors in front of them. In a subsequent task, participants in the high-self-focus conditions were more likely to use self-referential pronouns, more likely to say that stereotyping is wrong, and less likely to engage in stereotyping.

Although stereotype suppression theory has shown some promise, other studies have indicated that it can backfire and produce higher levels of prejudice. The problem arises when the act of trying to avoid thinking prejudiced thoughts ironically makes these thoughts even more salient in one's mind, and thus potentially more influential in one's behavior. Known as "suppression rebound," this problem is easy to recognize in other aspects of life. Consider dieting: people try to suppress their desire for unhealthy food, yet the more they try not to think about, say, ice cream and fried chicken, the more they do end up thinking about those foods (and probably eating them). The same logic applies to efforts to avoid stereotypic thinking about social groups. In some experiments, increasing levels of self-focus or receiving instructions to avoid prejudiced thinking led to lower levels of out-group bias *initially*, but then produced higher levels of bias on later tasks (compared to a no-exposure control condition).[12]

The probability of rebound effects is much less clear in the case of prejudice toward blacks because strong social norms may lead whites to be especially vigilant in keeping racially prejudiced thoughts at bay. The studies demonstrating rebound effects used out-groups that are more socially acceptable targets of prejudice, such as skinheads.[13] In other words, trying to suppress stereotypic thinking may always make stereotypes more salient in people's minds, but this may still leave a choice about whether to rely on those stereotypes when evaluating out-groups, at least where consciously held attitudes are concerned. Consistent with this idea, some experimental evidence has found that receiving instructions to avoid stereotyping of blacks reduces racial stereotyping without producing rebound effects later on.[14]

The 2008 presidential campaign offered an excellent opportunity to see if stereotype suppression theory works in the real world. Exposure to news coverage highlighting ongoing racism in American society should have spurred whites, according to the theory, to engage in self-reflection about their own potentially racist attitudes, thus producing declines in racial prejudice.

COVERAGE PROMOTING RACIAL UNITY

Another possible explanation for the Obama effect is that exposure to the campaign reduced racial prejudice because of Obama's rhetoric emphasizing the identity that whites and blacks share as Americans. As one news story noted, "[Obama] has sought to emphasize connections among Americans rather than divisions."[15] According to the common in-group identity model, another prominent theory of prejudice reduction, focusing attention on the national identity that whites and blacks have in common has the potential to undercut intergroup bias.[16] During the campaign, Obama called for unity among Americans, regardless of race, ethnicity, or other social divisions. In Berlin, on July 24, 2008, he proclaimed that "the walls between races and tribes, Christians and Muslims and Jews cannot stand. These now are the walls we must tear down." Little more than a month later, during his acceptance speech at the Democratic National Convention, he referenced a Martin Luther King Jr. speech emphasizing unity, proclaiming, "We cannot walk alone." As Obama elaborated, "What the people heard instead—people of every creed and color, from every walk of life—is that, in America, our destiny is inextricably linked, that together our dreams can be one."

Indeed, during the campaign, journalists replayed a similar message from Obama's speech at the 2004 Democratic National Convention: "There is not a Black America and a White America and Latino America and Asian America. There's the United States of America." This theme recurred in Obama's victory speech on the night of November 4, 2008:

> It's the answer spoken by young and old, rich and poor, Democrat and Republican, black, white, Hispanic, Asian, Native American, gay, straight, disabled, and not disabled. Americans who sent a message to the world that we have never been just a collection of individuals or a collection of red states and blue states. We are and always will be the United States of America.

Might exposure to this sort of unifying rhetoric help to reduce white racial prejudice? The answer ironically lies in the same psychological process thought to initiate prejudice: the tendency of people to favor members of their own social group over outsiders.[17] The common in-group identity model proposes reducing prejudice by using in-group favoritism to lead people to view both their in-group and the out-group as part of a single, superordinate group. When it is successful, the lines between groups are redrawn to create a new in-group that includes both groups. In the context of the 2008 campaign, Obama's rhetoric of American unity may have led whites and blacks to see themselves *less* as members of different racial groups than as members of a single nation.

Both observational and experimental studies have examined the potential benefits of promoting a common in-group identity,[18] though many provide evidence that could be interpreted through multiple theoretical frameworks.[19] Some use cross-sectional surveys to show positive associations between reductions in prejudice and perceptions of in-group and out-group members as belonging to a single overarching group.[20] However, such correlational evidence provides a weak basis for causal inference, particularly in this case given the strong potential for reverse causality.

Nonetheless, three fully randomized experiments have demonstrated that perceiving a common in-group identity can in fact lead to improved intergroup attitudes.[21] One study employed the "minimal group" paradigm to first create group division and then either encouraged participants to continue to view themselves as members of two different groups or as members of a single overarching group.[22] Participants first took part in a series of tasks designed to make them feel like members of different groups, such as breaking into teams, wearing team T-shirts, and solving problems with their team. Despite the short time frame of the study, these tasks created a sense of group identity, including bias favoring members of their own in-group over the out-group. The groups were then brought together, and half sat at the same table, put on the same T-shirts, and received a new group name that they would all share. The other half sat at different tables and retained their initial group T-shirts and their separate group names. Consistent with the theory, the participants who were encouraged to see their two groups as parts of a single overarching group displayed less bias against participants who had initially been members of the out-group.

Although this evidence is promising, minimal group experiments are likely to underestimate the difficulty of reducing prejudice in the real world, where group identities are forged early in life, have long histories of antagonism, and experience ongoing conflicts—as with racial prejudice in the United States. It is thus encouraging that a more recent experiment found that drawing whites' attention to their national American identity reduced racial bias in policy attitudes, compared to a condition that drew attention to their racial identity.[23] Similarly, a separate experiment found that exposure to a newspaper editorial arguing that affirmative action in higher education benefits *all* students through increased diversity improved attitudes toward blacks, relative to a portrayal emphasizing past discrimination against blacks.[24] In sum, prior evidence suggests that focusing attention on a superordinate identity shared by both whites and blacks can lessen racial prejudice. Thus, exposure to Obama's American unity rhetoric during the 2008 campaign may have encouraged whites to view themselves and blacks as members of a single American in-group.

COVERAGE DRAWING ATTENTION TO RACE

Another possible explanation for declining white prejudice in 2008 is that simply drawing attention to the topic of race may be enough to produce this effect. The campaign included an unusually large number of explicit references to race (for example, "black" and "African American"). By drawing attention to race, one theory suggests, the 2008 campaign may have short-circuited prejudiced thinking and reminded whites of racially egalitarian social norms. According to Tali Mendelberg's implicit-explicit model, mentioning race explicitly reminds whites of their consciously held racially egalitarian views, thus inhibiting racially biased thinking.[25] In the absence of explicit references to race, this theory suggests that most whites remain unaware of their prejudiced attitudes because they operate largely on a nonconscious level.

Another theory similarly advocates drawing explicit attention to race, but for an entirely different reason. The categorization model suggests that positive feelings toward individual out-group members are more likely to generalize to more positive feelings toward the out-group as a whole when the group identity of the out-group members is highly salient.[26] Put another way, if the out-group member is perceived as an individual rather than as a representative of the out-group, then attitudes about the out-group member may not generalize to the out-group as a whole. Drawing explicit attention to group identities promotes generalization by strengthening the psychological link between the individual out-group member and the out-group; this is thought to be especially important when the out-group member is counterstereotypical and thus more likely to be dismissed as unrepresentative of the out-group.[27]

According to this theory, exposure to a highly counterstereotypical black exemplar should promote reductions in racial prejudice only if the coverage includes explicit references to race, lest whites fail to generalize from Obama to blacks as a group. Drawing explicit attention to race within this context should have strengthened the psychological connection between Obama and the category "African American" during the 2008 campaign, thus leading to improved views of African Americans.

An alternative theory, however, makes exactly the opposite prediction. Decategorization theory suggests that bringing up race focuses attention on intergroup differences. Conversely, downplaying group identity and instead focusing on the personal characteristics of out-group members leads in-group members to see them as fundamentally "just like everyone else."[28] Within this framework, intergroup contact produces beneficial effects by reducing the salience of group identities.[29] Learning personal details about out-group members ought to promote "individuation," that is, perceiving the out-group as comprising a diverse set of individuals. The more diverse the out-group is perceived to be, the less useful stereotypes become for describing it. If decategorization occurs, then mass public exposure to Obama should be more likely to reduce racial prejudice the *less* race is mentioned.

The categorization and decategorization theories obviously make different predictions about the role of explicit racial references during the 2008 campaign, but both theories suggest that the presence or absence of such references is a critical moderator of effects on attitudes toward out-groups. In contrast, exemplification through mediated intergroup contact does not require moderation by direct references to race. We turn next to a more detailed examination of the coverage of Obama to determine the extent of support for these alternative explanations.

THE CONTENT ANALYSIS

Each of the theories of media influence described in this chapter locates responsibility for the declines in white racial prejudice during the 2008 campaign in a somewhat different type of campaign coverage. Exemplification theory suggests that the sheer amount of coverage of Obama made him the most salient black exemplar in the minds of whites. According to stereotype suppression theory, coverage that explicitly discussed racism prompted whites to feel self-conscious about their racial attitudes. The common in-group identity model purports to show that coverage promoting a shared American identity led whites to view blacks as fellow in-group members rather than as outsiders. Finally, any coverage that referred to race explicitly may have been beneficial in prejudice reduction either by simply short-circuiting unconscious racism, as suggested by the implicit-explicit model, or by promoting generalization from counterstereotypical perceptions of Obama to African Americans in general, as suggested by the categorization model.

To examine which theory better explains change over time in white racial attitudes, we need measures of change over time in each type of campaign coverage. For this purpose, we relied on the largest available database of national media sources in the United States. This massive database, known as the Lydia System, was produced by nightly scraping of content from all U.S. news sources that are available on the Internet.[30] On a daily basis, a computer program "spidered" web pages from more than two thousand online U.S. news sources and downloaded all of this content to a large mainframe computer.

Next, a natural language processor took the raw text and produced numbers corresponding to a given search. For instance, we asked the database to provide the total number of daily references to a given search term, such as "Barack Obama," as well as to all logical variations of that term. The downside of using such an immense amount of raw data was that we were limited to less complex search terms with a small number of keywords. The ability to directly assess the reliability and validity of the search terms on the exact same body of text was also limited because copyright laws precluded retaining this huge amount of raw copyrighted material after the stories were scored by natural language processing.

For validation purposes, we employed a much smaller database, Lexis-Nexis, which allowed for long Boolean search terms and full-text output. Reading the actual stories facilitated analyses of reliability and validity with human coders. Although the results from the two databases would be expected to differ somewhat because they provide different amounts and forms of text, one would expect a strong correspondence between them. Indeed, as we report in appendix D, we found a high degree of reliability and convergent validity, consistent with prior research.[31]

Lexis-Nexis is not suitable for analyses of change over time in coverage because the raw data as provided by this service are not comparable. Whereas the system we used provides the total number of qualifying references for a given search, Lexis-Nexis returns the number of "hits," an undefined metric that varies across media sources.[32] As a result, apparent changes in the amount of coverage over time are confounded with variations between media sources in how hits are counted. For some news sources, hits correspond to the total number of news articles that mention given search terms; in other cases, hits refers to the total number of program episodes including a qualifying mention; still other entities use even more varied units of analysis.

For cross-sectional analyses, these limitations are not as problematic because such comparisons hold whatever metric is used constant (though some media sources are still weighted more than others because of a smaller unit of analysis). In fact, the longer Boolean searches allowed in Lexis-Nexis may produce better cross-sectional estimates of the amount of each type of coverage than the Internet-based system. So while we use nightly spidering of the Internet for our analyses of change over time, we use Lexis-Nexis to characterize the cumulative amount of each type of coverage across the campaign period.

THE AMOUNT OF EACH TYPE OF COVERAGE

Because our focus has been on television coverage, our estimates of total amounts of coverage were based on the thirty-two most-watched political television programs that are available in the Lexis-Nexis database. Figure 5.1 shows the overall amount of each of the four relevant types of coverage across the campaign period: (1) overall coverage of Obama, (2) coverage of Obama mentioning race, (3) coverage of Obama mentioning racism, and (4) coverage of Obama emphasizing racial unity.

Relative to the other three subcategories, there was a huge amount of overall coverage of Obama during the campaign. Nearly every politically relevant television program covered Obama substantially on every day throughout the fall. But notably, most of this coverage did not explicitly mention race. Only about 22 percent of the coverage of Obama included an explicit reference to race in some form. Even less coverage discussed racism—only about 10 percent of Obama coverage in total. Finally, it is worth noticing in figure 5.1 the minuscule amount of coverage mentioning racial unity. Despite Obama's repeated use of this campaign theme, only about 1 percent of campaign coverage included Obama's rhetoric promoting a shared American identity between whites and blacks. Although there were some high-profile examples of unity coverage, overall there was clearly too little coverage of this theme to explain the decline in white racial prejudice during the campaign.

Was there was enough emphasis on race or racism in this coverage to have an impact on white racial attitudes? Or was the sheer amount of coverage of

Figure 5.1   The Relative Amount of Each Type of Coverage

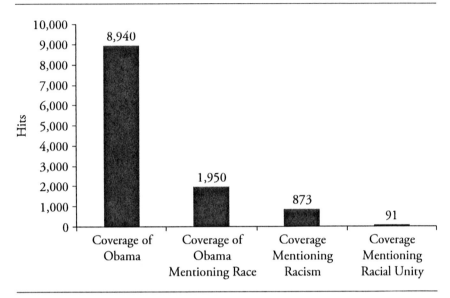

Source: Lexis-Nexis.
Note: The figure presents the number of hits for each type of coverage from Lexis-Nexis searches of political television shows for the period July 17, 2008, through January 31, 2009.

Obama alone responsible for the decline in racial prejudice? To answer these questions we turn next to an examination of the impact of change over time in exposure on change over time in racial prejudice.

THE IMPACT OF CAMPAIGN COVERAGE

Isolating the impact of each type of coverage on individual racial attitudes requires combining the data from our content analysis with our individual-level measures of media exposure to the campaign. In our earlier analyses, we found that the best measure of exposure to the campaign was a simple count of how many television programs including coverage of the campaign were viewed regularly by each person. In chapter 4, we demonstrated that increases over time in political television viewing led to over-time declines in racial prejudice. In other words, increases in individual exposure to the Obama campaign helped to reduce racial prejudice. In these additional analyses, we combine exposure data with the content analysis to isolate which *aspect* of the campaign coverage produced these beneficial effects.

To recall, each individual's interview date within the wave was randomly assigned; as a result, the coverage they experienced in between waves was somewhat different for each. This allowed us to match daily measures of each type of campaign coverage with respondents' interview dates within each wave. We used coverage viewed on respondents' interview dates rather than over a longer time frame because the theories of influence suggest that *recent* exposure exerts a disproportionate influence on attitudes toward out-groups. To be sure, we are not suggesting that only coverage from respondents' interview dates was influential; indeed, the amount of coverage of Obama on any given day was highly correlated with the previous day's coverage, as well as with coverage two days prior to that. Beyond a few days, however, the autocorrelations drop off precipitously, indicating that coverage varied considerably during the campaign. Because we had no a priori expectations about the exact time lag, we also created measures that averaged coverage on respondents' interview dates with several preceding days, producing two-day, three-day, four-day, five-day, six-day, and seven-day moving averages. We found extremely similar results from each of these measures; thus, for simplicity's sake, we present only the results using coverage from respondents' interview dates.

If the impact of changes over time in political television exposure depended on the type of coverage to which individuals were recently exposed, then changes over time in the amount of exposure should be moderated by the extent of change over time in the relevant type of exposure. In other words, we would expect a significant interaction between these two variables. So, for instance, if coverage of Obama helped to reduce racial prejudice, then increases over time in political television viewing should be particularly influential when accompanied by increases over time in the amount of coverage of Obama. A negative and statistically significant interaction would indicate that increases over time in exposure to coverage of Obama led to reductions in racial prejudice. As in our previous analyses, we rely on fixed-effects models comparing each respondent to himself or herself at an earlier point in time. We also include a wave variable representing the average effects of the passage of time to capture the sum-total effects of other factors that changed during the campaign.

Was it particular types of media coverage of the campaign that produced changes in levels of white racial prejudice? To test the hypotheses outlined here, we took the analyses in chapter 4, including change over time in political television viewing, and added the variables representing each type of coverage

Table 5.1   The Effects of Change in Exposure to Coverage
of Obama on Change in White Racial Prejudice,
Wave 3 to Wave 5

	(1)	(2)
Wave 3 to wave 5	−1.99***	−1.99***
	(0.28)	(0.28)
Number of political TV shows viewed	−11.38***	−6.22#
	(2.77)	(3.73)
Coverage of Obama	1.77	5.31*
	(1.50)	(2.27)
Number of shows × Coverage of Obama		−21.55*
		(10.41)
Constant	11.03***	10.20***
	(0.83)	(0.92)
Sample size	1,956	1,956

Source: 2008 NAES Panel Survey.
Note: The table presents unstandardized fixed-effects regression coefficients, with standard errors in parentheses. All of the independent variables range from 0 to 1. Both models control for within-person change in the order in which the racial groups were asked about.
***p < 0.001; *p < 0.05; #p < 0.10

and their interactions with political television viewing. We began by testing the most general type of coverage—the total amount of coverage of Obama— and then assessed whether each of the more specific aspects of coverage of Obama produced any additional effect. The analyses here present the significant changes we uncovered from wave 3 to wave 5.

Table 5.1 replicates our analyses of the impact of overall exposure to coverage of Obama. As a baseline from which to assess the interaction between change in political television viewing and change in coverage of Obama, column 1 of table 5.1 presents a fixed-effects model that includes just the main effects of these two variables. Consistent with our findings in chapter 4, increases over time in political television viewing produced significant declines in white racial prejudice.

Column 1 of table 5.1 also includes the main effect of change in coverage of Obama. We did not have specific expectations about the impact of this variable, given that its impact should logically depend on the extent of individual political television viewing. Perhaps unsurprisingly then, column 1 shows a small and nonsignificant coefficient for change in the amount of coverage of Obama.

Column 2 of table 5.1 adds the interaction between change in political television viewing and change in the amount of coverage of Obama. Consistent with exemplification theory, the interaction is negative and statistically significant, indicating that increases over time in political television viewing produced especially large declines in racial prejudice when accompanied by increases over time in coverage of Obama.[33] In other words, whites who experienced greater exposure to coverage of Obama exhibited much larger declines in racial prejudice compared to whites who experienced less exposure to coverage of Obama.

Exposure to coverage of Obama of any kind appears to have led to reductions in racial prejudice, just as exemplification theory predicts. But is it possible that this overall influence is driven by one of the specific subtypes of coverage we have outlined? We already know that only a minuscule amount of coverage mentioned racial unity, so this type of coverage obviously cannot explain the decline in white racial prejudice. Was coverage emphasizing race or racism influential above and beyond over-time variations in the sheer amount of coverage of Obama?

Table 5.2 addresses the question of whether Obama coverage explicitly mentioning race was especially important to the Obama effect. Column 1 of table 5.2 provides the appropriate baseline model showing the effects of change over time in exposure to coverage of Obama. In column 2, we add the interaction between change in political television viewing and change in coverage mentioning race. The interaction coefficient is *not* statistically significant, suggesting that exposure to coverage mentioning race did not produce any additional impact on change in white racial prejudice above and beyond the sheer amount of coverage of Obama. One might wonder whether multicollinearity due to the inclusion of multiple interactions is suppressing the impact of coverage that mentioned race; however, even in a model with only the one interaction, coverage mentioning race fails to reach statistical significance.

In table 5.3, we address another alternative explanation—that coverage discussing racism caused the declines in racial prejudice by prompting whites to engage in self-reflection about their own racial attitudes. We tested this hypothesis following the same analytic strategy employed in table 5.2. Column 1 of table 5.3 presents the baseline model, and in column 2 we add the interaction between change in political television viewing and change in coverage discussing racism. The interaction coefficient is positive, but only marginally

Table 5.2   The Effects of Change in Exposure to Coverage of Obama Mentioning Race on Change in White Racial Prejudice, Wave 3 to Wave 5

	(1)	(2)
Wave 3 to wave 5	−1.99***	−1.98***
	(0.28)	(0.28)
Number of political TV shows viewed	−6.22#	−6.14
	(3.73)	(3.95)
Coverage of Obama	5.31*	4.63
	(2.27)	(3.60)
Number of shows × Coverage of Obama	−21.55*	−22.04
	(10.41)	(15.71)
Coverage of Obama mentioning race		1.06
		(3.89)
Number of shows × Coverage of Obama mentioning race		0.21
		(16.56)
Constant	10.20***	10.29***
	(0.92)	(0.98)
Sample size	1,956	1,933

Source: 2008 NAES Panel Survey.
Note: The table presents unstandardized fixed-effects regression coefficients, with standard errors in parentheses. All of the independent variables range from 0 to 1. Both models control for within-person change in the order in which the racial groups were asked about.
***$p < 0.001$; *$p < 0.05$; #$p < 0.10$

significant ($p < 0.10$), suggesting little impact from coverage discussing racism. Moreover, the positive sign of the coefficient indicates that, if anything, coverage discussing racism may have produced small *increases* in racial prejudice. This would be consistent with stereotype suppression rebound, whereby exposure to antiracist messages backfires by increasing the salience of preexisting prejudices. As in the previous analysis, we assessed the potential for collinearity due to including multiple interactions in the same model, but the results were again unchanged when the model included only the interaction between television viewing and coverage of racism. Overall, we found little to no evidence in support of our plausible rival explanations.

To the extent that coverage mattered, it mattered only that it involved Obama, and not whether race, racism, or racial unity was discussed.

Table 5.3   The Effects of Change in Exposure to Coverage Mentioning Racism on Change in White Racial Prejudice, Wave 3 to Wave 5

	(1)	(2)
Wave 3 to wave 5	−1.99***	−1.87***
	(0.28)	(0.31)
Number of political TV shows viewed	−6.22#	−7.55*
	(3.73)	(3.79)
Coverage of Obama	5.31*	5.26*
	(2.27)	(2.29)
Number of shows × Coverage of Obama	−21.55*	−22.38*
	(10.41)	(10.42)
Coverage mentioning racism		−1.18
		(1.39)
Number of shows × Coverage mentioning racism		9.79#
		(5.32)
Constant	10.20***	10.33***
	(0.92)	(0.95)
Sample size	1,956	1,974

Source: 2008 NAES Panel Survey.

Note: The table presents unstandardized fixed-effects regression coefficients, with standard errors in parentheses. All of the independent variables range from 0 to 1. Both models control for within-person change in the order in which the racial groups were asked about.

***$p < 0.001$; *$p < 0.05$; #$p < 0.10$

OBAMA AS EXEMPLAR

The fact that exposure to the 2008 presidential campaign helped to reduce levels of white racial prejudice is useful information, but from a theoretical standpoint what is far more important is understanding *how* the campaign produced these effects. Public and scholarly debate about the effects of media portrayals of blacks and other social groups has raged for decades, but with little beyond speculation on which to base its claims. As a result, scholars often disagree about the predicted direction of influence from the same media content.[34]

In this chapter, we have furthered understanding of the prejudice-reducing impact of the 2008 campaign bye testing four theories, each relying on a different mechanism of influence. Exemplification theory pointed to the importance of the sheer amount of coverage of Obama as a counterstereotypical black exemplar. Stereotype suppression theory suggested that coverage that included direct discussion of racism would be most influential. The common in-group identity model pointed to coverage of Obama's rhetoric of racial unity between blacks and whites. The implicit-explicit model and the categorization model emphasized the importance of the increase in coverage explicitly mentioning race.

To evaluate these various theories we combined self-reports of individuals' political television exposure with a large-scale content analysis of campaign coverage and found that only the sheer amount of coverage of Obama had a significant impact in reducing prejudice. The other kinds of content—coverage addressing racism, race, or racial unity—did not have the predicted influence. As suggested by others examining the "Obama effect," exemplification theory appears to offer the most parsimonious explanation for the campaign's effect on white racial prejudice. This conclusion is also consistent with experimental evidence gathered after the campaign showing that exposure to Obama caused declines in racial prejudice, at least temporarily.[35]

Of course, it is possible that some other aspect of campaign coverage that we missed caused the decline in racial prejudice, though this seems unlikely. Any alternative explanation would need to involve a type of coverage that not only could reduce racial prejudice but also occurred in sufficient quantities to do so at the national level among diverse segments of the population, including among conservatives and in conservative media.[36] The countless images of Obama and his family countering negative racial stereotypes most clearly fit these criteria.

PART III

Epilogue: White Racial Attitudes After the 2008 Campaign

CHAPTER 6

Whatever Happened to the Obama Exemplar?

The most important question posed by the systematic change in white racial attitudes observed in our earlier chapters is whether this change was sustained over time. Did white racial attitude remain more positive, or did they lapse along with the optimism of this unique moment in history? Given the centrality of Obama coverage to the exemplification effects that lessened prejudice toward African Americans, the persistence of this coverage and its effects is a central concern in evaluating the longer-term prospects for reducing prejudice. As described in chapter 4, exemplification changes people's attitudes by altering the exemplars that most easily come to mind when they are asked to think about a larger category of people. Whatever is easily accessible in memory is thus more likely to come to mind. Humans are cognitively limited, and expediency trumps thoroughness, so people base their assessments on easily available, though not necessarily representative, exemplars rather than on the totality of all people within a given category.

In this chapter, we consider what exemplification theory suggests about how exposure should affect levels of prejudice after the election. Studies of the persistence of the exemplification effect are limited, but the assumption has been that it is a comparatively—some even say "exceedingly"—short-lived effect that relies on recency of exposure.[1] From this perspective, any given exemplar's influence may be limited to the time prior to when it is superseded by new exemplars, a time one assumes would be relatively short given the nature of ongoing media coverage. Once exemplars are replaced by newer, more recent exemplars, the influence of the old ones should wane as attention is directed elsewhere.

However, the appropriate theoretical prediction is not entirely that simple because recency is not the only factor that enhances the accessibility of exemplars; characteristics of the exemplar and how it is presented in the media also matter. Basically any factor that raises the salience of an exemplar gives it greater influence on judgments because it makes that exemplar more accessible. For example, emotional exemplars have disproportionate influence because they are more accessible in memory than unemotional exemplars.[2]

What this account suggests in the case of the Obama exemplar is that in a rapidly changing media environment the accessibility of exemplars could change relatively quickly if the flow of exemplars changes abruptly. On the other hand, in the real world people's judgments are often influenced in a particular direction and remain that way for relatively long periods of time, precisely because the flow of exemplars is relatively stable in mass media. Owing to routine news practices, drastic changes in the nature of coverage are few and far between. Media coverage of African Americans tends to disproportionately focus on negative exemplars involving poverty, crime, welfare, and broken families.[3] Coverage of this kind results in the chronic accessibility of negative exemplars, and thus more persistent effects of accessibility on attitudes.

The promising patterns of lessened racial prejudice described in part II made us eager to find out whether the counterstereotypical presence of Barack Obama in the media was sustained in coverage after the election. The story we have told to explain what happened during the 2008 campaign suggests that what happened next should depend crucially on Americans' ongoing levels of exposure to Obama or possibly other positive and negative black exemplars. Because exemplification effects are inherently fleeting and ephemeral, the increasingly positive associations with blacks that many white Americans developed should require ongoing exposure in order to be sustained.

For better or worse, elections are notably unusual periods of time for media coverage of political figures. For a few months while offices are being actively contested, there is a huge amount of sustained coverage of political leaders. Unfortunately, we know little about what happens afterward. The attention of both scholars and the public generally turns elsewhere after an election concludes.

Using yet another wave of panel data collected in 2010, we tested the same hypothesis about the impact of media coverage of Obama, this time during the post-election period through the 2010 midterm elections.[4] We looked closely at both how media coverage and public opinion changed during the post-election period in order to understand longer term trends.

A much smaller sample size for this recontact study made it impossible to take advantage of randomly assigned interview dates, as in the original panel, so our efforts were focused instead on maximizing the number of responses and the demographic representativeness of our subsample. To facilitate statistical comparisons over time, we focused on respondents who had participated in most or all of the previous waves of the study. Altogether, 83.7 percent of the panelists contacted agreed to participate in the 2010 panel wave.

To alleviate potential concerns about attrition, we replicated the analyses discussed in chapter 2 for this additional wave of data. As shown in appendix C, 2010 panel respondents were somewhat more educated and older than the panelists interviewed during the campaign. We also ran the same panel conditioning analysis as before, this time using prejudice in 2010 as the outcome of interest. We found no significant effects of either the total number of prior waves completed or the number of prior waves that had included the prejudice items. Overall, these analyses reassured us that attrition and conditioning had no major effects on the sixth wave of this panel.

POST-ELECTION EXEMPLIFICATION EFFECTS?

To begin, we used the additional wave of panel data from 2010 to evaluate whether the predictions of exemplification theory held up two years after the election. In chapters 4 and 5, the results consistently suggested that when individuals' exposure to Obama increased, their associations of blacks with negative attributes declined. This effect occurred above and beyond any secular trend toward decreasing prejudice. But what about two years later? Did change in Obama exposure from 2008 to 2010 retain the same implications for white racial prejudice? To test this proposition, we used panel data from the post-election wave in 2008 and compared them to answers to the same questions in 2010. As in our analyses of the pre-election data, we used fixed-effects analysis to test the hypothesis that increases in exposure should correspond to declines in prejudice.

Table 6.1 shows the results of this analysis. Given the much longer time lag between waves in this analysis and the short-term theoretical nature of the effects previously documented, we were not confident that we could capture

Table 6.1   The Effects of Change in Political TV Exposure on
            Change in White Racial Prejudice, 2008 to 2010

	Change in Racial Prejudice
Number of political TV shows viewed	−4.41*
	(2.05)
Wave 5 to wave 6	1.61***
	(0.21)
Constant	9.67***
	(0.57)
Sample size	3,222

Source: 2008 NAES Panel Survey; 2010 RSF Recontact Study.
Note: The table presents unstandardized fixed-effects coefficients, with standard errors in parentheses. The model controls for change in the order in which the racial groups were asked about.
***p < 0.001; *p < 0.05; all two-tailed

the cumulative effects of changes in Obama exposure on racial attitudes with waves two years apart. Nonetheless, as shown in table 6.1, the findings are virtually identical to what we saw in chapter 4. Just as seen in the first column of findings in table 4.1, increases in the number of political programs that a given individual viewed resulted in significant decreases in racial prejudice. In addition, the size of the coefficient corresponding to change from 2008 to 2010 (−4.41) is virtually identical to the coefficient in table 4.1 (−4.51). Despite the fact that our sample in 2010 was smaller, changing media consumption was still significantly tied to changing levels of prejudice toward blacks. Those with the largest increases in the number of programs viewed regularly exhibited a drop of just over four points on the prejudice scale. As discussed at length in chapter 4, although the extent of this change may be modest by most standards, by historical standards it is relatively large.

Was this change driven particularly by those whose level of exposure to Obama dropped? Of course, after the election almost everyone's exposure to Obama dropped to some extent because political television featured him less often. In our model, any across-the-board impact is captured by the dummy variable representing change from one wave to the next; that dummy variable does indeed suggest an overall decline. But the prediction in this case would be that those individuals whose exposure to Obama decreased the most would also increase the most in prejudice from 2008 to 2010.

As discussed in chapter 4, fixed-effects analysis produces conservative estimates of these relationships relative to many other statistical techniques. We use it here because by focusing on individual-level change, we avoid the problems of selection and of cross-sectional associations that are mistakenly assumed to be causal. The persistence of the relationship between media exposure and prejudice is especially impressive in this light. Although this approach does not rule out all possible rival interpretations (particularly interactions between personal characteristics and changes in exposure), it rules out the most obvious ones, such as the idea that less prejudiced people who already liked Obama exposed themselves to more televised politics after his election. By focusing on individual-level change over time, we see that changes in viewing go hand in hand with changes in views of blacks.

The one clear difference between the results shown in tables 4.1 and 6.1 is the sign of the dummy variables indicating the direction and extent of change in racial prejudice that was independent of changes in media exposure. During the election, both wave coefficients were negative and statistically significant, indicating that, above and beyond the effects of media exposure, prejudice was declining. In contrast, as shown in table 6.1, during the post-election period the coefficient was significant and positive, indicating increasing prejudice. So although increases in media exposure corresponded with declines in prejudice, the overall trend appears to have been in the opposite direction, that is, toward increased levels of prejudice.

To further clarify what happened in the post-election period, we plotted simple mean comparisons over time including the three original closely spaced waves and the fourth wave gathered shortly before the midterm elections in 2010. Figure 6.1 summarizes racial prejudice at each wave of the panel survey, ignoring the more fine-grained distinctions based on the interview date within the wave.

The overall pattern is stark. The sharp drop in prejudice witnessed during the 2008 campaign was followed by an increase. This shift back toward more stereotypical perceptions of blacks did not return the aggregate level of prejudice back up to where it was before the election, but it came very close. In fact, it came close enough to be statistically indistinguishable from the pre-election level, at least with the reduced power of our smaller 2010 sample. So although our results from both periods of time were entirely consistent with exemplification effects of media and exposure to Obama continued to discourage prejudice, the overall trend was toward *increasing* levels of prejudice.

Figure 6.1   Change in White Racial Prejudice from 2008 to 2010

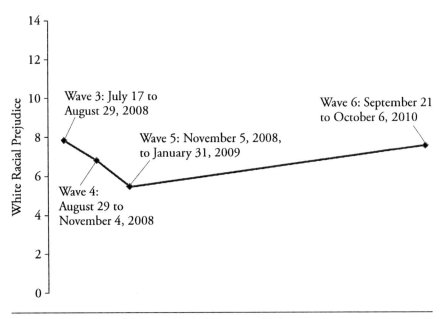

Source: 2008 NAES Panel Survey; 2010 RSF Recontact Study.
Note: White racial prejudice ranges from 0 to 100, where higher positive values indicate higher levels of prejudice. The figure relies on the 1,533 white respondents who completed the prejudice measures on all four waves.

How can this be? To understand how increases in exposure may correspond to decreases in prejudice and yet prejudice increases on the whole, we turned next to an analysis of over-time changes in exposure.

POST-ELECTION EXPOSURE TO OBAMA

How much did people continue to see Obama in their living rooms after the election? After a presidential election is over and the inauguration has passed, presidents do not disappear from the news, but politics no longer takes center stage. After Obama's election, we looked at two forms of change that could jeopardize the extent of public exposure to positive black exemplars: a drop in levels of individual interest in and viewing of political programming, and a decline in the extent of media coverage of Obama's day-to-day activities.

In our panel spanning post-election 2008 through the fall of 2010, a declining interest in politics was evident in virtually every kind of indicator. The viewing of television newscasts fell abruptly and significantly after the election, along with the viewing of political talk shows and newsmagazines. The only type of program that sustained an audience the same size after the election as before was political satire. Regardless of the type of measure examined and which portion of the panel we analyzed, the story was the same. The mean number of political programs viewed declined and the relative preference for news (the reverse of relative entertainment preference) declined significantly from before the election to afterward. Once the suspense of the election was over, Americans were simply watching fewer political programs.

But even if people had watched the same number of programs as before, was Obama as omnipresent in coverage as he was before the election? Because the president commands a large amount of media attention no matter what he says or does, it is possible that levels of coverage of Obama did not change substantially. Nonetheless, our prediction was that journalistic attention would decline substantially post-election.

Once in office, presidents no longer have the capacity that they once did to produce television coverage on demand.[5] Viewership of presidential addresses has declined since the advent of cable because people have more attractive television options from which to choose. Moreover, television networks no longer automatically cover every presidential speech and action. Although important national events can certainly trigger an onslaught of presidential coverage, this is not the norm. Moreover, even though a president's efforts to "go public" by taking his arguments directly to the American people can boost coverage, these are temporary blips in the ongoing background hum of American politics outside of election periods. Overall, Americans today are probably seeing less of their president than they did thirty to forty years ago.[6]

But does coverage of the winning presidential candidate still drop off once he is in office? Given that there is suddenly only one winner to focus on, rather than two or more candidates, the anticipated pattern is not entirely straightforward. To examine the extent to which our prediction of substantially less coverage was borne out, we tracked the extent to which Obama was mentioned in television news broadcasts from June 2008 (pre-election) through September of 2010, leading up to the midterm elections. Figure 6.2 shows the number of Obama mentions that occurred weekly. There are two obvious coverage peaks: one during the week of the 2008 election itself, and

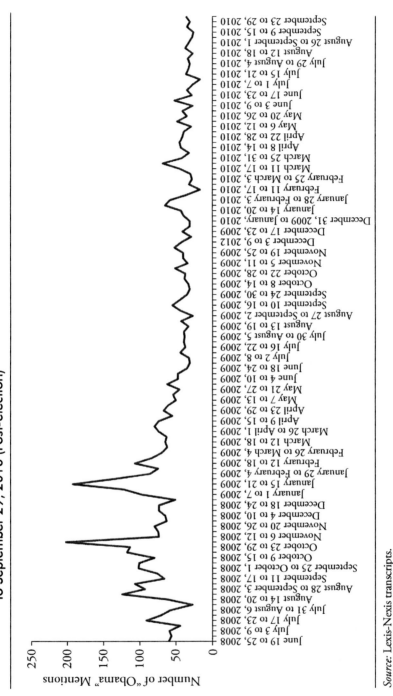

Figure 6.2 The Change in Obama Coverage from June 19, 2008 (Pre-election), to September 29, 2010 (Post-election)

Source: Lexis-Nexis transcripts.

Note: Entries represent the number of Obama mentions per week in the three network broadcast news programs.

a second during inauguration week. Before the election, the amount of coverage of Obama steadily built up to the election day peak. Shortly after the inauguration peak, coverage took a nosedive and settled at levels lower than in the pre-election buildup.

What this pattern suggests is that elections are unique periods of time for exposure to presidents (in the case of incumbents) and for presidents-to-be. Television covers presidents far more when they are still candidates than it does once they are elected. Television coverage during the campaign period is far more substantial than it is during the actual presidential administration.

Combining what we have learned from survey data regarding political television viewership patterns before and after the 2008 election with patterns of coverage during the same time period makes one thing clear: the American public was far less likely to see Obama after the election than they were during it, both because they were watching fewer political television programs and because the same programs were no longer covering him as much.

This finding begs the question of which other black exemplars were prominent in the news from 2009–2010 that may have displaced the Obama exemplar. In general, coverage of African Americans in the news centers on specific events and individuals rather than on blacks as a demographic group or issues related to African Americans more generally. The Pew Research Center's Project for Excellence in Journalism carried out an extensive content analysis of news coverage during the year following the election and found that less than 2 percent of coverage included explicit mention of African Americans.[7] Of that coverage, one story easily exceeded the prominence of the Obama administration the year following the election: the arrest of black Harvard University professor Henry Louis Gates by a white police officer. As Pew notes, this story "accounted for nearly four times more African-American-related coverage" than did either of the two biggest national issue stories. In July 2009, Gates was mistakenly suspected of trying to break into his own home. A local police officer in Cambridge, Massachusetts, responded to a 911 caller who reported two men breaking and entering. In reality, Gates had just returned from an overseas trip and found the front door to his home jammed shut. He and his driver then tried to force it open. Gates was arrested by the responding officer and charged with disorderly conduct.

Although accounts of their interaction differ, Gates accused the white officer of racism, and the incident generated a national debate about whether or not it represented an example of racial profiling by police. Thereafter, talk shows were rife with commentary from representatives of the African American community such as Michael Eric Dyson, the Reverend Jesse Jackson, Al Sharpton, and Cornel West. Conservative programs paid more attention to the incident than liberal ones,[8] and President Obama was heavily criticized by conservative media for weighing in on the matter by saying the local police "acted stupidly" when he was not witness to the event. Later that month Obama attempted to smooth things over by inviting both the officer and Gates to a private meeting at the White House, dubbed the "Beer Summit." Interestingly, this incident generated more coverage of racism as an issue than any aspect of the 2008 campaign other than Obama's "A More Perfect Union" speech, which he gave in the wake of claims about antiwhite racism by Obama's former pastor, the Reverend Jeremiah Wright.

The Pew report examined portrayals of blacks in coverage with explicit references to race and in stories that "related in a significant way to African Americans," which required that 25 percent of the story be about blacks. Arguably, then, the report excluded the large portion of coverage of African Americans that either did not mention race explicitly or did so without focusing much of the story on African Americans. We can only speculate about what this other coverage looked like during the year after Obama's election, but if prior academic research is any indication, then most portrayals of blacks were probably negative. As one recent study concluded, "African Americans typically occupy roles as poor people, loud politicians, and criminals on network news."[9]

The pattern shown in figure 6.2 suggests that the prominence of Obama in the media dropped off quickly after the election and inauguration, thus making that particular exemplar less salient. With declining coverage of the Obama exemplar, and no particularly positive exemplars of equal salience to replace it, it is not surprising that positive perceptions of blacks should wane during the first two years of Obama's administration. Importantly, the coefficient in table 6.1 reflects both the extent to which *increases* in exposure corresponded to *decreases* in prejudice and the extent to which *decreases* in exposure corresponded to *increases* in prejudice.

If our explanation for what we have observed is correct, then it should be the case that in the three waves of panel data surrounding the election, the effect we observed was driven by increases in exposure that produced decreases in prejudice, whereas the effect observed during the first two years of the Obama administration is accounted for mainly by significant decreases in exposure that drove increases in white prejudice. After all, most people's exposure to

Table 6.2   The Effects of Increases and Decreases in Political
             TV Exposure on Change in White Racial Prejudice
             During the 2008 Obama Campaign

Number of political TV shows viewed	−4.29* (2.07)	
Increases in the number of political TV shows viewed		−9.76** (3.11)
Decreases in the number of political TV shows viewed		1.02 (3.19)
Constant	−0.98*** (0.13)	−0.64** (0.19)
Sample size	2,065	2,065

Source: 2008 NAES Panel Survey.
Note: The table presents unstandardized fixed-effects coefficients, with standard errors in parentheses. The independent variables are coded to range from 0 to 1. Each model controls for change in the order in which the racial groups were asked about. A chi-square test showed that the difference between the coefficients for increases and decreases was significant (chi-square = 5.17, $p < 0.05$).
***$p < 0.001$; **$p < 0.01$; *$p < 0.05$; all two-tailed

Obama was increasing in the time leading up to the election, then decreasing during the first two years of the administration. Because only a *change* in the status quo flow of exemplars should produce changes in whites' racial stereotypes, periods of rapid change in coverage are particularly important.

To test this explanation we separated our exposure variables into two different measures, one indicating increasing exposure to Obama, and the other indicating decreasing exposure. We then reran our fixed-effects analyses of change over time, putting these variables into the models simultaneously. Tables 6.2 and 6.3 present the results of these analyses for the period surrounding the election and the post-election period, respectively.

In the first column, we show the average overall effect of media exposure. In the second column, we separate this effect into the impact of increases versus decreases. As shown in table 6.2, the significant negative coefficient observed in the original panel occurs because increases in political media exposure during the election correspond to decreases in racial prejudice. The relatively small number of people whose exposure decreased did not change significantly in racial prejudice. Interestingly, the coefficient corresponding to the impact of

Table 6.3   The Effects of Increases and Decreases in Political TV Exposure on Change in White Racial Prejudice During the First Two Years of the Obama Administration

Number of political TV shows viewed	−4.41*	
	(2.05)	
Increases in the number of political TV shows viewed		1.14
		(4.24)
Decreases in the number of political TV shows viewed		−7.64*
		(2.98)
Constant	1.61***	1.33***
	(0.21)	(0.28)
Sample size	3,222	3,222

Source: 2008 NAES Panel Survey; 2010 RSF Recontact Study.
Note: The table presents unstandardized ordinary least squares (OLS) coefficients, with standard errors in parentheses. The independent variables are coded to range from 0 to 1. Each model controls for change in the order in which the racial groups were asked about. A chi-square test showed that the difference between the coefficients for increases and decreases was not significant (chi-square = 2.24, $p = 0.13$).
***$p < 0.001$; *$p < 0.05$; all two-tailed

increasing exposure during this period was even larger than the original estimate, suggesting a nine-point decline in prejudice scores among those whose program viewing increased the most.

As shown in table 6.3, the same summary coefficient for media exposure meant something quite different in the post-election period. As shown in the second column of table 6.3, in this case the significant negative effect was driven by decreases in exposure, which corresponded to increases in prejudice. Given that almost everyone declined in their exposure in the post-election period, this is precisely what one would predict: as the barrage of Obama imagery dropped off dramatically, so too did the more positive associations that whites had with African Americans. Unless coverage changes, people's underlying associations remain relatively stable. But given sufficient reinforcement, these associations can change even in a relatively short period of time.

PLAUSIBLE ALTERNATIVES

Although this evidence makes a great deal of sense in light of our theoretical explanation for what happened, several plausible rival hypotheses are worth further examination. As with any observational study, no matter how powerful, there are always threats to any given interpretation that should be seriously considered. Stable individual differences are accounted for in these models by focusing strictly on individual-level change. But changes over time that spuriously correspond to changes in media exposure could be misleading if they drive both changes in viewing habits and changes in white prejudice. So what are the other possibilities?

First, some have posited that the evidence we have observed is really a story about post-election conservative media turning increasingly critical in its coverage of Obama. After the honeymoon was over, the feel-good historical moment had passed, and the business of governing was at hand, so it is plausible that the tone of coverage changed. But according to exemplification theory, criticism of Obama's politics should be irrelevant; what matters is that he was presented as a stand-up guy, directly contrasting with whites' traditionally negative stereotypes of blacks.

To evaluate whether criticism of Obama and his presidency encouraged more prejudiced attitudes among viewers, we broke down media exposure into programs consistently viewed as liberal or conservative, as described in chapter 4. Then, in addition to using the overall change in media exposure in our models, we also included indicators of the proportion of media exposure that was conservative or liberal. If viewing conservative programs caused negative changes over time in racial attitudes, it would lend credence to the hypothesis that it was not simply exposure to Obama but uncomplimentary exposure that mattered for changing prejudice levels. Moreover, it would suggest that something other than purely exemplification was at work.

Consistent with the evidence in chapter 4, there was no evidence that conservative media promoted more negative views of blacks via political coverage critical of the Obama administration. Instead, as shown in table 6.4, media exposure of various partisan flavors had roughly equivalent impacts on over-time changes in prejudice. Regardless of how we looked at these data, we found no evidence of partisan media effects in the rebounding levels of racial prejudice evident in the post-election period.

These results were particularly surprising to us in light of the extensive media coverage that the "birther" movement received. After the election, many on the far right supported some variety of conspiracy theory asserting that Obama was not in fact a natural-born U.S. citizen and thus was not eligible to be president. These theories were widely discussed in conservative media during this time. Nonetheless, we found no evidence that these efforts to associate Obama with foreignness promoted traditional African American

Table 6.4   The Effects of Change in Partisan Media Exposure
               on Change in White Racial Prejudice During the
               First Two Years of the Obama Administration

Wave 5 to wave 6	1.63***
	(0.21)
Number of political TV shows viewed	−5.46*
	(2.17)
Proportion conservative	0.66
	(0.93)
Proportion liberal	1.32
	(0.91)
Proportion neutral	0.55
	(0.74)
Constant	9.30***
	(0.64)
Sample size	3,222

Source: 2008 NAES Panel Survey; 2010 RSF Recontact Study.

Note: The table presents unstandardized fixed-effects regression coefficients, with standard errors in parentheses. All of the independent variables range from 0 to 1. Each model also includes the order in which the racial groups were asked about.

***$p < 0.001$; *$p < 0.05$; all two-tailed

stereotypes. Indeed, here as in previous evidence, liking Obama seemed to be entirely beside the point of being affected by his exemplar.

In addition to the argument that coverage changed qualitatively as well as quantitatively during this period, the most obvious large-scale change going on was the economic collapse. As mentioned briefly in chapter 4, the decline in prejudice witnessed from the summer of 2008 through the inauguration in January 2009 was particularly surprising given the dramatic economic downturn that transpired during that same period. Although people knew the economy was in bad shape by the summer preceding the election, their sense of economic decline only intensified after that, as evidenced by continuously declining assessments of national economic conditions as well as declining assessments of their personal financial conditions.

It would be easy to understand how such a large and wide-reaching economic threat might overshadow the subtle associational learning suggested by exemplification theory. According to realistic group conflict theory, feelings toward out-groups should suffer when economic times are hard and resources are scarce. When people feel economically threatened, their animosity toward out-groups increases because of the tendency to rally around the in-group at the expense of the out-group—or at least so the argument goes. Evidence supporting the theory of realistic group conflict has been mixed at best.[10] Further, as discussed in chapter 4, analysis of the panel data from during the campaign shows that changes in economic perceptions—whether of personal finances or of the national economy—were completely unrelated to changes in racial prejudice at that time. In the aggregate as well as at the individual level, changes in economic perceptions moved in the opposite direction predicted by theories of realistic group conflict: whereas perceptions of economic conditions worsened during the 2008 campaign, prejudice declined during the same period. Moreover, including perceived changes in the economy in these models did not change any of the estimated effects of mass media.

But what about the post-election relationships estimated in table 6.1? The aggregate pattern is again inconsistent with the direction of change: perceptions of the economy significantly improved during the same period in which prejudice worsened, precisely the opposite of what realistic group conflict would predict. Nonetheless, to evaluate the individual-level evidence to ensure that changing economic perceptions did not produce mis-estimations of the media's impact, we reran our panel models to include change in people's perceptions of the national economy and change in perceptions of one's own personal finances.

As shown in table 6.5, changing perceptions of personal finances were unrelated to changes in prejudice during the 2008 campaign. Perceptions of changing national economic conditions likewise showed no significant relationship with change in prejudice. In the post-election panel, however, a shift toward more optimistic perceptions of national economic conditions significantly predicted a decline in prejudice, just as realistic group conflict would predict. Those whose concern about the economy eased during this period were less likely to increase in their level of in-group favoritism. Notably, however, this relationship had no bearing on the size or significance of the impact of changing media exposure. Both during the campaign and during the first two years of Obama's presidency, those whose media exposure increased were those whose racial prejudice decreased. This effect was consistent despite the fact that the overall trend was toward improvement during the original panel but in the direction of increased prejudice during the first two years

Table 6.5   The Effects of Change in Economic Perceptions on Change in White Racial Prejudice

	During the 2008 Campaign	During the First Two Years of Obama's Presidency
Number of political TV shows viewed	−4.28* (1.89)	−4.61* (2.07)
Perceptions of national economy	−0.36 (0.25)	−0.55** (0.16)
Perceptions of personal finances	0.23 (0.21)	0.20 (0.19)
Wave 3 to wave 4	−0.95*** (0.26)	
Wave 3 to wave 5	−2.10*** (0.26)	
Wave 5 to wave 6		2.14*** (0.26)
Constant	10.46*** (0.61)	9.56*** (0.62)
Sample size	2,038	3,163

Source: 2008 NAES Panel Survey; 2010 RSF Recontact Study.
Note: Table entries show unstandardized fixed-effects coefficients, with standard errors in parentheses. Each model also includes the order in which the racial groups were asked about.
***$p < 0.001$; **$p < 0.01$; *$p < 0.05$; all two-tailed

of Obama's presidency. Far from overshadowing the media's impact on the tendency toward white in-group favoritism, economic change had at most a very small impact, while media exposure was consistently linked to declines in whites' tendency to negatively stereotype blacks.

To ensure that we left no stone unturned and no possible relationship with economic change went unnoticed, we ran numerous additional models to evaluate whether those whose attitudes toward the economy were particularly negative at a given point in time were more likely to be affected by media coverage. Given that economic perceptions were already extremely negative by 2008, it seemed quite plausible to us that perhaps we were observing "floor effects." In other words, there was relatively little room for change toward more negative economic perceptions to matter. However, we found no evidence to this effect. Regardless of individuals' assessment of their personal

Figure 6.3   Change in White Perceptions of Race Relations, Wave 3 to Wave 6

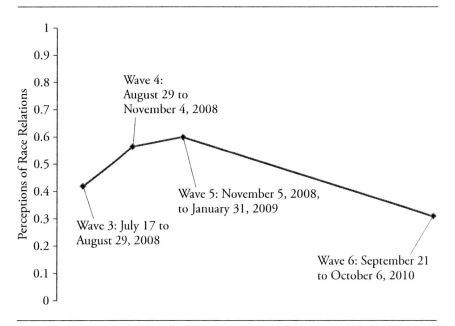

Source: 2008 NAES Panel Survey; 2010 RSF Recontact Study.

Note: The perceptions of race relations index ranges from −2 to 2, where negative values indicate a pessimistic view and positive values indicate an optimistic view. The figure relies on the 3,032 white respondents who completed the measures on all four waves.

finances or of the nation as a whole, media coverage had the same effects on the extent of white in-group favoritism.

POST-ELECTION TRENDS IN PERCEPTIONS OF RACE RELATIONS

In part because the 2010 findings for racial prejudice indicated some slippage back to previous levels of white in-group favoritism, we also wanted to follow up on the trend toward improved perceptions of race relations. As discussed in chapter 3, increasingly positive perceptions of race relations appeared to go hand in hand with reductions in prejudice during the campaign; this suggests that the increase in prejudice by 2010 might have been accompanied by declining optimism about race relations as well.

In figure 6.3, we add our 2010 estimate for the index of perceived race relations to extend the overall trend. As shown, the overall pattern is indeed similar to that of racial prejudice. White perceptions of race relations improved significantly during the 2008 campaign, but by 2010 that perception of improvement had diminished. This finding struck us as quite surprising: both symbolically and in reality, the election of a black president represents the willingness of a substantial number of whites to support a black candidate. Despite the fact that Obama did not receive a majority of whites' votes, the sheer fact that he became a viable candidate for a major party nomination was a surprise to many Americans who had argued that the United States was "not ready" to elect an African American as president.

It is important to remember from chapter 3 that this trend toward rosier perceptions of race relations started long before Obama was actually elected, so it cannot be purely a function of electing an African American as president. Obama's primary victories and successful nomination by the Democratic Party could account for the pre-election trend, but our data points are primarily after the effects of his selection as nominee should have been registered. The impact of specific events does not provide a good explanation for what we observed. In addition, changes in white perceptions of race relations do not appear to be driven by changing amounts of exposure to Obama the way that our racial prejudice indicators were. Although they followed a similar trajectory over time, we must look elsewhere, beyond exemplification theory, to explain these trends.

We can offer no definitive theory in this regard. Nonetheless, it is worth noting that although the three indicators in the perceived race relations index moved up and down together in the pre-election panel, the pattern in the post-election period is somewhat different. Relative to when the panel began in the summer of 2008, perceptions of race relations "today" were still significantly more positive in 2010. But interestingly, perceptions of race relations "in the last ten years" and perceptions of the future of race relations "in the next ten years" both indicated greater pessimism in 2010 than in the summer of 2008. Our best guess is that this reflects a sense among whites that having a black president represents a uniquely positive period in race relations that is neither likely to be repeated again soon nor an accurate reflection of the past.

In addition to assessing change in white Americans' perceptions of race relations, we also wanted to follow up on the trend among African Americans. Chapter 3 indicated that both white and black perceptions improved during the 2008 campaign. Given that white perceptions became more pessimistic during the first two years of the Obama presidency, we naturally wondered

Figure 6.4   Change in Black Perceptions of Race Relations,
Wave 3 to Wave 6

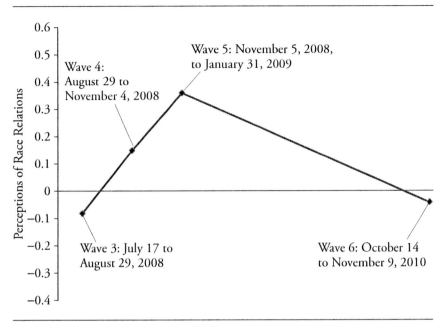

Source: 2008 NAES Panel Survey; 2010 ISCAP Recontact Study.
Note: The perceptions of race relations index ranges from −2 to 2, where negative values indicate a pessimistic view and positive values indicate an optimistic view. The figure relies on the 601 black respondents who completed the measures on all four waves.

whether blacks' perceptions moved in the same direction. To find out we recontacted a representative subsample of blacks in the fall of 2010 under the auspices of the Institute for the Study of Citizens and Politics at the University of Pennsylvania.[11]

Figure 6.4 shows the trend for the index of perceived race relations from the summer of 2008 through the fall of 2010 among African Americans. The first thing to notice is the astonishing improvement in blacks' perceptions of race relations during and immediately after the 2008 campaign—a jump more than twice the size of the changes we observed among whites. But matching the increasing optimism of 2008 is the significant decline in optimism over the next two years. Indeed, blacks' perceptions of race relations in the fall of 2010 were statistically indistinguishable from their perceptions in the summer of 2008.

THE FLEETING IMPACT OF EXEMPLARS

Do the results in this chapter suggest that the earlier impact of Obama on racial attitudes was purely symbolic? Setting aside for the moment the issue of what it means to be symbolic, two conclusions stand out from the many analyses conducted in this chapter. First, there is extensive empirical evidence consistent with exemplification theory and the importance of mediated inter-group contact. Psychologists have long noted evidence of exemplification in highly controlled laboratory studies, and it is equally and consistently supported in these observational data. Whether examined at the level of individual or aggregate change, increases in the prevalence of the Obama exemplar corresponded to decreases in racial prejudice, and decreases in its prevalence corresponded to increases in racial prejudice. From a theoretical perspective, we appreciate the consistency in our findings across multiple settings and extensive amounts of panel data. Evidence from the two years following the election only provides additional support conforming to these expectations.

On the other hand, as citizens who care about reducing racial prejudice and negative out-group attitudes more generally, we found our results extremely disappointing. Obama's campaign and election clearly had no long-term, sustained impact on whites' racial attitudes, at least not as of 2010. If something as monumental as electing a black president cannot sustain a positive impact on racial attitudes, whites' attitudes would seem to be highly intransigent.

We think this would be the wrong lesson, however, to draw from this evidence. This is not to say that the improvement was not real, nor that the reversion back was not real. The patterns we observed are far too systematic to represent random noise in whites' judgments of blacks. Moreover, these changes are far too large to represent the kinds of fluctuations that are commonly seen over relatively short periods of time.

What our results underscore is the relative malleability of racial prejudice, at least by comparison to the conventional wisdom in public opinion research. The ongoing assumption has been that racial attitudes form in early childhood and then crystalize, so that prejudice remains stable throughout adulthood. But as others have pointed out, the seeming stability of public opinion may in fact reflect the stability of the information to which citizens are exposed.[12] The same appears to be true of racial attitudes, which may rarely deviate owing to the consistent nature of media portrayals of blacks. The 2008 campaign showed that when an unusual event intervenes and produces a positive shift in portrayals, then racial prejudice declines; when the hoopla of the election ends and positive portrayals become less dominant, then racial prejudice increases. These changes may surprise scholars who think of racial prejudice as immutable in the short term, but they are utterly consistent with numerous studies of exemplification, which find that brief exposure to black exemplars causes modest changes in attitudes toward blacks. If what it takes to sustain more positive white attitudes toward blacks is large-scale, more persistent awareness of positive African American exemplars, then this avenue for change is hardly intractable.

Moreover, our findings suggest that in an era when most white Americans' exposure to blacks is primarily via mass media, it matters a great deal which African Americans get covered most heavily. Observers have been commenting for years about the paucity of positive images of blacks in the media. Most such research has emphasized the problems associated with threatening images of black criminals rather than the impact that positive exemplars might have. Laboratory studies have already provided convincing causal evidence that making positive exemplars salient lessens the tendency to attribute negative characteristics to blacks. The unusual amount of coverage received by America's first African American presidential nominee from a major political party is a highly unusual case merely because of the extremity and suddenness of its impact. The usual relatively stable flow of black exemplars was interrupted by suddenly extensive coverage of Obama that notably contrasted with widely held stereotypes. Media fascination with the Obama family enhanced its potential for positive influence on the white American public.

The optimistic take in this chapter is that racial stereotypes are to some degree malleable in the short term; prejudice cannot be eliminated overnight, of course, but positive movement is possible in a span of time that is far shorter than has been previously assumed. The negative side of this is that it appears to take a great deal of extensive coverage of a counterstereotypical black individual to change the many negative associations with blacks that are held by white Americans. Even during the 2008 campaign, when coverage of Obama was at its peak, that coverage still had to compete with the many other images of blacks that continued to reinforce racial stereotypes. High-profile African Americans may balk at the idea of being role models for other blacks, as Charles Barkley so famously argued in his widely viewed Nike advertisement. But by virtue of being in the public eye regularly and accessible in the minds of whites, they are most certainly serving as exemplars for white Americans forming their views of what black Americans are like.

CHAPTER 7

Implications for the Study of Racial Attitudes

Few events have surprised pundits and political scientists as much as the 2008 election of Barack Obama as president of the United States. Once Obama was reelected in 2012, it became even more difficult to recall the extreme skepticism that had accompanied his candidacy. At the commencement of the primary season in late 2007, the idea that a black man would be elected president seemed highly implausible to most Americans, precisely because of the long-standing history of racism in this country. Strangely enough, by the end of that election season, many of those same observers expressed great surprise that racial prejudice had influenced people's choice of candidate.

In reality, few people would have predicted otherwise. The negative effects of racial prejudice on vote choice in biracial election contests were not new or unique to this election. As a result, we found it unfortunate that the bulk of research on Obama's election in 2008 was focused on prejudice as a cause of vote choice. In many ways, it is quite peculiar that political science research has focused almost exclusively on racial prejudice as a *cause* of voting behavior or policy attitudes rather than as a problem in its own right. The center of gravity in this literature could just as easily have been racial prejudice as a dependent variable, with a focus on those aspects of political arrangements or policies that serve to increase or decrease levels of racial prejudice. This oversight is especially surprising given that public opinion research represents the largest area of research on prejudice. Nonetheless, this literature has almost nothing to say about what increases or reduces prejudice.[1]

Instead, prejudice has been assumed to be a largely stable attribute throughout the life course that is unlikely to change.[2] According to this line of thought:

> Even if the words and actions of black incumbents do not fit racial stereotypes, whites can use an array of tactics to try to maintain their stereotypes and create cognitive consistency.[3] They can ignore events that disconfirm their current views or discount contradictory evidence as an exception to the rule.[4]

Based on this expectation, scholars' most optimistic hope has been to try to limit the impact of racial prejudice on political attitudes and behaviors, but not reduce prejudice itself. For example, in *Changing Minds, if Not Hearts*, James Glaser and Timothy Ryan take the intransigence of racial prejudice as a given and thus try to reduce racial conflict through alternative framing of political choices. "Our tests do not claim to have changed underlying sentiments but only (though often pivotally), the way they come to bear on politics."[5]

We suggest that the significance and novelty of the 2008 election is not that racial prejudice prevented some whites from voting for Barack Obama or that racial sympathy led some to support him. Prejudice has undoubtedly influenced vote choice in every political race pitting an African American against a white American. Instead, the significance of the 2008 election lies in how the campaign itself affected the way many whites thought about blacks more generally. Because of persistent racial segregation in many areas of life, relatively few white Americans have frequent interactions with African Americans. As a result, their images of this group are often based on secondhand impressions that reach them largely through mass media. Our results show, for the first time, that exposure to a black candidate through the media improved whites' impressions of blacks.

In addition, this study makes several contributions that go beyond the specific events and time period that we have studied. Perhaps most surprising is evidence of the short-term malleability of racial attitudes. As the airwaves were flooded with counterstereotypical images for a period of time, white Americans came to have fewer negative associations with African Americans. Unfortunately, these more positive views did not last, in large part because the amount of attention that the media and the American public paid to presidential politics dropped off precipitously after the election. Obama was certainly still featured in news coverage, but not as much as other prominent black exemplars across the media spectrum.

Although our overall story line is a disappointing one, the silver lining is that in both laboratories and the real world we have now seen convincing evidence that positive black exemplars can improve whites' attitudes toward blacks. Interestingly, this same theory may account for some previous findings as well. For example, Zoltan Hajnal's discovery of a declining racial divide when a city has recently been governed by a black mayor could be explained in a variety of ways.[6] He suggests that racial divisions decline because whites learn from being governed by a black mayor that their interests will not suffer under black leadership. While this is certainly plausible, it is also possible that cities have experienced a surge in local media coverage of positive black exemplars as a result of electing a black mayor. That local news is by far the most popular form of news makes such an explanation even more plausible. Although Hajnal's research can speak only to aggregate increases in positive sentiment toward blacks, our individual-level data confirm that individual exposure to positive black exemplars through media is tied to less stereotypical attitudes.

ARE POSITIVE EXEMPLARS REALLY POSITIVE?

The fact that it is good for white racial attitudes when intelligent, accomplished blacks appear on the television screen may seem obvious to those who are not familiar with ongoing debates over what kind of media would best discourage racial prejudice. In scholarly circles, however, the verdict has been confused and contradictory at best. It may seem self-evident that a positive portrayal should produce more progressive attitudes toward blacks, whereas a negative portrayal should encourage more prejudicial views, but scholars regularly disagree about whether the same content should produce beneficial or detrimental effects.

Central to this debate over what kind of black exemplar is best for race relations has been a tension between those whose criteria for judgment focus directly on how whites feel about blacks, whether they stereotype them in negative ways, and so forth, and those who focus instead on support for government policies designed to redress racial inequality. The quite logical fear in this case is that the accomplishments of one highly prominent African American, Barack Obama, might overshadow the ongoing need for policies to improve the plight of African Americans more generally. As one commentator put it, many supporters "worry that Obama's historic achievements may make it harder to rally support for policies designed to combat racial discrimination, racial inequities, and urban poverty. They fear that growing numbers of white voters and policymakers will look at Obama . . . and decide that the work of eradicating racial discrimination and ensuring equal opportunity in this country is largely done."[7]

In 1994 the General Social Survey began asking Americans if "because of past discrimination, blacks should be given preference in hiring and promotion" or whether it "is wrong because it discriminates against whites." Around nine in ten whites have opposed hiring preferences every time the question has been asked, so the policy is clearly unpopular among whites. But blacks' policy attitudes have changed over time as well. Support for affirmative action policies is on the wane among blacks.[8] The policy was originally quite popular among blacks, but support decreased from a little over 60 percent in 1994 to just 45 percent in 2008. Likewise, whereas white support for government aid to blacks has been low and has held steady since the 1970s, support among blacks has dropped substantially, from a little over 70 percent in 1975 to a little over 40 percent in 2008.

Ironically, concerns of this kind have produced a great deal of ambivalence among blacks as well as among progressive whites about whether Obama's election is such a good thing for blacks after all.[9] Such reactions put African Americans in a hopeless bind: if they achieve great things and do well in the world, they are simultaneously undermining the cause by convincing whites that discrimination no longer holds blacks back. On the other hand, if they do not accomplish great things, then they are yet another negative exemplar for African Americans, reinforcing negative stereotypes in white minds.

When it comes to televised portrayals of blacks, further controversy stems from the frequent suggestion that the blacks shown on television are too well off relative to the actual status of blacks in general, with too many doctors and lawyers, at least in the fictional television world.[10] When it comes to nonfictional television, such as news programs, most studies argue precisely the opposite, that is, that blacks are shown predominantly as negative exemplars and in positions of inferiority.[11]

Unfortunately, there is no comprehensive source of information about television content—either fictional or nonfictional—that would allow us to address this question in a comprehensive, ongoing way. As a result, there is also considerable confusion about the impact of television on racial attitudes.

For example, some have explicitly lauded *The Cosby Show* as paving the way for Obama's election by providing a rare counterstereotypical portrayal of blacks.[12] At the same time, others have criticized the show for discouraging progressive policy views by failing to portray the poverty and discrimination afflicting many blacks.[13]

Do well-off blacks implicitly suggest that blacks themselves are solely responsible for their group's condition? It is plausible that the representations of blacks in *The Cosby Show* promoted both less negative stereotypes of blacks *and* the perception that blacks could get ahead if only they tried hard enough. However, research supports only one of these two conclusions to date: according to experimental evidence, as well as the results of our study, exposure to highly successful blacks leads whites toward weaker endorsements of negative stereotypes, including the stereotype that blacks are less hardworking than whites. Importantly, in experimental studies images of successful blacks have also led whites to perceive *more* discrimination against blacks as a group.[14] Trend data show that most white Americans are well aware of racial inequality and the fact that African Americans lag behind whites economically. Around 80 percent of whites consistently rate blacks as less well off than whites, and that percentage has remained basically stable over time, as has the gap between black and white incomes.[15]

It is not entirely clear why being reminded of successful African Americans leads whites to perceive greater discrimination against blacks and not toward less of a desire to help them. Most likely this occurs because thinking about blacks in more positive terms (for instance, as nice, hardworking, and intelligent) also produces greater sympathy for blacks as victims of discrimination. Galen Bodenhausen and his colleagues suggest that this pattern could result from the fact that whites use their overall attitude toward blacks as a heuristic, so "any contextual factor that produces a more favorable attitude toward African-Americans may also produce more favorable related political beliefs (for example, that African-Americans are indeed the victims of unfair discrimination)."[16] Indeed, a recent experimental study found that exposure to counterstereotypical images of black media characters undercuts perceptions of blacks as lazy, leading to more positive *overall* feelings about blacks and, consequently, increased support for affirmative action (relative to those exposed to stereotypical images).[17] To the extent that exposure to positive black exemplars produces more favorable views of blacks overall, this shift may produce more favorable responses on a wide range of issues related to blacks.

We suspect that people are affected in positive or negative ways by exemplars because the processing of television content occurs at a level that encourages simple associations of positive/negative characteristics with blacks when they are repeatedly paired together. The more positive/negative a person's feelings about blacks, the more positive/negative their feelings about the government policies designed to help them. In contrast, situations in which more positive feelings toward blacks would cause whites to have more negative feelings about a policy designed to help blacks would require far more cognitively involved processing. While there is a logic to it, we suspect that most whites do not think all that hard about these issues, particularly when processing television.

WHAT MAKES AN EXEMPLAR POSITIVE?

Assuming that we have laid to rest for the moment the question of whether media coverage of successful blacks is actually good for white racial attitudes, we turn next to what our research suggests about what constitutes a "positive" exemplar for purposes of encouraging more egalitarian racial attitudes. If mediated intergroup contact and media coverage of positive black exemplars is to serve as a means of improving white racial attitudes, then it is essential to know what precisely makes an exemplar positive. As we have seen from our results, it is not quite as straightforward as saying that an exemplar must be "well liked." Even Republicans who did not like Obama at all were moved toward less prejudicial stereotypes from exposure to his campaign, even when exposure occurred through conservative television programs.

We suggest that what makes an exemplar positive is highly specific to historical context and the negative stereotypes associated with a particular minority group. For an African American to serve as a positive exemplar today, he or she must counter the most prominent negative stereotypes associated with blacks. The most prominent negative stereotypes include the idea that blacks are lazy, violent, complaining, and less intelligent than whites. As a result, a black man would be a positive exemplar if he comes across as hardworking, intelligent, and nonthreatening, the opposite of the stereotypical "angry black man."

Aside from his many accolades, Obama accomplished this during the campaign in large part by avoiding the topic of race altogether. With the exception of his speech in Philadelphia after the anger expressed by his pastor, the Reverend Jeremiah Wright, Obama's campaign did not voluntarily address the issue of race head on. As one journalist described it, "Mr. Obama has walked this tightrope about as well as anyone could, has answered racial questions when they have been unavoidable, but has visibly striven not to be defined or confined by them, to make his candidacy about something other than his paint job and his culture."[18]

Obama's "More Perfect Union" speech in Philadelphia was widely praised, but it was an exception as far as his campaign was concerned. Race was otherwise not a central focus. Even when bigotry was openly expressed on the campaign trail, it was quickly swept under the rug and not brought to public attention. For example, when Obama campaign offices were vandalized in the state of Indiana during the primary season (including bomb threats, smashed windows, and racial epithets spray-painted on the walls), Obama campaign officials said that they did not want to make a big deal of the incidents, and these events received very little press attention.[19]

The decision to avoid race appears to have been quite deliberate. As a result, what is perhaps most striking about the election coverage from 2008 is just how little race and racism were discussed, as noted in chapter 5. As one conservative noted, because Obama was reluctant to claim racism, it made him far less threatening to whites; he clearly did not fit the "complaining" stereotype: "What really set him apart from the people who had roughly the same views he did is that he did not demonize the people on the other side of the dispute. . . . He was not the sort to accuse people of being racist for having different views of affirmative action."[20] Shelby Steele made a similar observation shortly after the election:

> Obama is what I have called a "bargainer"—a black who says to whites, "I will never presume that you are racist if you will not hold my race against me." Whites become enthralled with bargainers out of gratitude for the presumption of innocence they offer. . . . Thus whites became enchanted enough with Obama to become his political base. It was Iowa—95 percent white—that made him a contender. Blacks came his way only after he won enough white voters to be a plausible candidate.[21]

In a period of great interracial anxiety, Obama relieved whites' anxieties by strategically avoiding conversations about race. Instead, he engaged in what psychologists would characterize as a "recategorization" strategy, emphasizing a superordinate category to which different groups all belong—specifically, a national American identity—in order to unite blacks and whites in support of him. Obama explicitly avoided running as the "black candidate" to the extent that this was possible, instead emphasizing the commonalities that "we" all share as Americans. Former Secretary of State Colin Powell suggested that Obama's campaign approach was unprecedented compared to previous black politicians:

> Here's the difference in a nutshell, and it's an expression that I've used through-
> out my career—first black national-security adviser, first black chairman of the
> Joint Chiefs, first black Secretary of State. What Obama did, he's run as an
> American who is black, not as a black American. There's a difference. People
> would say to me, "Gee, it's great to be the black Secretary of State," and I would
> blink and laugh and say, "Is there a white one somewhere? I am the Secretary of
> State, who happens to be black." Make sure you understand where you put that
> descriptor, because it makes a difference. Obama . . . didn't run just to appeal to
> black people or to say a black person could do it. He's running as an American.[22]

Although chapter 5 found no direct evidence that Obama's rhetoric of unity was what encouraged less prejudice among whites, it probably con-tributed to making him less threatening to whites, and thus a more effective positive exemplar.

OPERATING UNDER THE RADAR

It is common to characterize racism in contemporary America as subtle, covert, latent, implicit, or unconscious. These terms all suggest an attitude that is somewhat hidden, or at least not expressed directly. But perhaps more importantly, these descriptors suggest that this bias is below people's level of conscious awareness, in contrast to the more overt forms of racism of the past.

In response to these characterizations, it is worth pointing out that blatant forms of racism have clearly not disappeared entirely.[23] These forms may exist to a much lesser extent than they once did, but they still exist. And regardless of whether prejudice is blatant or more subtle, the people who express these views are unlikely to view themselves as racist.

In evaluating our evidence on the impact of mediated intergroup contact, we were struck by the parallels between claims about the nature of racism in contemporary America and the important impact of media on racial attitudes that we have discovered. To the extent that what concerns us today is the kind of prejudice of which people are unaware, then our approach to addressing this problem ought to be similarly subtle. To the extent that discriminatory actions by whites are rooted in lingering negative associations, then these associations are not likely to be ameliorated by direct confrontation or accusation. In other words, for people who do not consider themselves prejudiced, interventions designed to address this issue head-on may not work and could even backfire.

Notably, people do not need to consider themselves prejudiced in order to be affected by the implicit associations conveyed in mass media. Moreover, people do not need to believe that television accurately represents the social world in order to be affected by the positive or negative associations that it continually presents. The cultivation of positive and negative associations occurs without people's awareness or permission. We found that direct coverage of racism made no apparent difference to racial attitudes in 2008. In addition, avoiding the subject of racism may have been an essential part of Obama's strategy for making himself nonthreatening to whites. Studies of nonmediated intergroup contact suggest that anxiety about interracial contact is one of the key factors preventing contact from having beneficial effects. Mediated intergroup contact, on the other hand, avoids the anxieties of face-to-face contact entirely. For this reason, it may be capable of even more beneficial effects than direct interactions. Perhaps exemplification works as well as it does because it is under the radar, unlike direct coverage of racism.

These characteristics make the role of media appear increasingly important in reducing people's implicit negative associations with blacks. We quite purposely say "people" here, rather than strictly whites, because both blacks and whites can suffer from the kinds of negative implicit associations that media cultivate.[24] Cultural stereotypes associating blacks with vice more often than virtue cannot help but influence the attitudes of both blacks and whites. As mentioned briefly in chapter 2, social psychologists have developed techniques of measuring unexpressed and unconscious associations by means of procedures such as the Implicit Association Test (IAT) and the Affect Misattribution Procedure (AMP). Although opinions differ as to whether these measures tap prejudicial attitudes, all agree that they tap latent associations between stimuli. So to the extent that people associate negative characteristics with African Americans as a result of seeing negative stimuli repeatedly paired with blacks, negative stereotypes are unlikely to change.

The key lesson to be learned from this study is that it matters a great deal how African Americans are prominently depicted in mass media. Thus, it is also important to systematically track how blacks are portrayed in the media. At present, we know of no efforts to track prominent black exemplars within either fictional or nonfictional media. There are occasional isolated studies of coverage involving blacks in local newscasts or of the portrayal of gays, blacks, and Hispanics in prime time, but to our knowledge there is no systematic effort to track which African Americans make the news and thus are made prominent in the minds of white Americans. Such an effort would seem essential for improving media's self-awareness of how blacks are portrayed and thus for improving the implicit associations of both white and black Americans.

Overwhelmingly, empirical research on race and media has emphasized the prevalent problem of negative racial stereotyping. The focus on negative effects is not surprising, but it results in scholars knowing little about whether beneficial effects may also accrue from positive racial exemplars. Research on media portrayals of race, dating back to Gordon Allport,[25] has focused almost entirely on the negative—the ways in which media cast blacks in a negative light and presumably serve to increase racial prejudice. Thus, what scholars have counted is how many blacks are shown as criminals, as violent, or as lazy. Only recently have scholars started to consider media as a means of prejudice reduction. To date most of that research has been conducted outside the United States and has used a more direct, pedagogical approach. For example, Elizabeth Paluck examined the effects of a yearlong radio soap opera in Rwanda that explicitly modeled intergroup conflict and reconciliation.[26] She found that, unfortunately, exposure to the program did not lead to any significant change in levels of prejudice, though social norms did move in a positive direction.

Few people ever receive as much media attention as a candidate for president of the United States. Because electing the leader of the free world is viewed as an unquestionably important matter, presidential candidates always receive heavy ongoing coverage of every aspect of their lives. This amount of coverage is highly unusual, and as we have seen, the ability to command such attention is also very temporary. For this reason, it seems doubtful that any one black exemplar will be likely to dominate the airwaves again as Obama did during the historical election of 2008. What will matter most instead is the aggregate flow of black exemplars in mass media and whether portrayals are on balance positive or negative. As the rise in prejudice after the 2008 campaign made clear, even an exemplar as widely covered as Obama could not override the status quo for long.

IS IT REALLY PREJUDICE REVISITED

As we discussed in detail in chapter 2, most public opinion research has centered on how best to measure prejudice. Disputes over appropriate measurement have unfortunately overshadowed what is clearly more important, which is change in more favorable directions. Regardless of whether one questions our use of the term "prejudice" to characterize our measure or prefers another term, there is little doubt that what we tap is important and consequential. Negative stereotypes play an influential role in social distance preferences such as neighborhood composition. Whites who hold more negative racial stereotypes are less willing to share neighborhoods with blacks.[27] Such whites are also more likely to oppose social policies targeted at helping African Americans and less likely to think that African Americans deserve help.[28] This tendency of whites who hold negative racial stereotypes extends to their evaluations of individual blacks as well.[29] Moreover, perceptions of even small differences in the positive and negative characteristics held by racial groups can cause differential treatment.[30] Finally, negative racial stereotypes influence whites' support for black candidates and government policies that aim to redress racial inequality.[31] In sum, negative stereotypes matter, and by this measure exposure to the Obama exemplar helped to reduce racial prejudice during the 2008 campaign.

MASS MEDIA AND RACIAL ATTITUDES

We hope that our findings will propel scholars to reconsider the general neglect of mass communication in producing and reducing racial prejudice. Research in this area may have been hindered by the failures of older media studies aimed at reducing prejudice through blatant antiracism messages—like the well-known "Mr. Bigot" studies that portrayed an over-the-top old man spouting racial slurs.[32] Consistent with what we now know about how mediated intergroup contact works, in those studies self-evidently antiracist messages did little to change racial attitudes.

More than half a century later, the view that media have little or no ability to alter racial attitudes still reigns in political science. Most studies of media impact remain rather limited in their aspirations.[33] Take, for example, the almost exclusive focus of research on media and race on how media exposure may activate or "prime" latent racial attitudes in political decisions. Yet as Donald Green and Rachel Seher point out, "The claim that mass communication shapes the salience of particular policy concerns is politically important, but much less so than the more forceful claim that communication creates or strengthens [racial] attitudes."[34]

Social psychologists, for their part, have long treated racial attitudes as changeable in the short term, as the voluminous research on intergroup contact and exemplar effects indicates. But given the relative amount of exposure to out-group members that people experience through mass media, it is puzzling that media have received so little attention.

Twenty years ago, Larry Bartels proclaimed that "the state of research on media effects is one of the most notable embarrassments of modern social science."[35] Unfortunately, this still seems to be true with regard to the study of media impact on stereotyping and prejudice. Although some experimental evidence has demonstrated the potential influence of media exposure on prejudice, our study represents one of the few to do so convincingly in a real-world setting. Ignoring the role of mass media is increasingly hard to defend given the demonstrated relevance of media portrayals to intergroup relations.

BEYOND THE OBAMA EFFECT

One remaining question raised by our study is whether the effects we observed in 2008 were repeated during the 2012 presidential campaign. On the one hand, the campaign once again produced a jump in coverage of Obama and public interest in politics, leading to an overall increase in exposure to the Obama exemplar. On the other hand, excitement over the historic nature of Obama's presidency had by then faded substantially, so there could easily have been less interest in his 2012 campaign than there was in 2008. It is also possible that exposure to Obama would have had a diminishing return as time wore on. As America's first black president, Obama had become less novel and unexpected, so the Obama exemplar could have had less subsequent impact on racial attitudes. As little as race was talked about during the 2008 campaign, it was talked about even less during the 2012 campaign. Of course, one could view the fact that Obama's race is no longer newsworthy as quite an achievement in itself.

As of this writing, data on the 2012 election are just being released, so scholars have not yet thoroughly examined changes in racial attitudes that may have occurred as a result of the surge in coverage during the Obama reelection campaign. Coverage of Obama naturally increased during the election period, and our preliminary assessment is at least consistent with

Figure 7.1   Change in White Racial Prejudice from 2008 to 2012

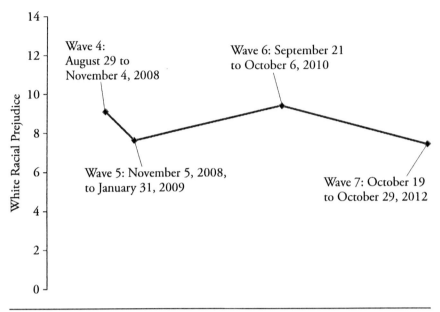

Source: 2008 NAES Panel Survey; 2010 RSF Recontact Study; 2012 ISCAP Survey.
Note: White racial prejudice ranges from 0 to 100, where higher positive values indicate higher levels of prejudice. The figure relies on the 684 white respondents who completed the prejudice measures on all four waves.

what exemplification would predict. Based on a new panel wave collected right before the 2012 election, white racial prejudice once again declined from the fall of 2010 through the 2012 campaign. Consistent with predictions and prior evidence, this decline was driven by improved attitudes toward blacks, with no change in attitudes toward whites. As shown in figure 7.1, the size of the decline in prejudice also appears strikingly similar in size—about two points—which is about the same size as the decline in prejudice during the 2008 campaign.

As we have noted many times in this book, the Obama effect is highly unusual insofar as one man (and his family) single-handedly changed the dominant image of blacks in mass media. However, an Obama effect on a smaller scale or from an ongoing flow of positive exemplars could become more frequent in years to come. Research on exemplar effects and intergroup contact suggests that changing negative stereotypes is actually much easier when exposure involves multiple positive exemplars; thus, exemplification effects could accumulate as more African Americans are featured as positive exemplars.

Importantly, the theory of mediated intergroup contact is not limited to blacks and racial attitudes. For example, exposure to highly successful female exemplars undermines gender stereotyping, and mediated contact with positive gay exemplars improves attitudes toward gay, lesbian, and transgender Americans.[36] Coincidentally, the voters in Wisconsin elected Tammy Baldwin as the first openly gay U.S. senator in 2012; she joined a historically large class of twenty women in the U.S. Senate. Exposure to many positive out-group exemplars—whether blacks, gays, women, or others—is growing in American politics. So, although the Obama effect may soon run its course, media coverage of salient out-group members will continue to play an important role in producing intergroup contact and influencing intergroup attitudes. We have barely scratched the surface in harnessing media's capacity to achieve these positive ends.

APPENDIX A

Benefits of Fixed-Effects Regression in Panel Analyses

In this book, we employ multiple waves of nationally representative panel data to document and explain changes in white Americans' racial attitudes during and after the 2008 presidential campaign. Because each individual was interviewed on at least three occasions, we were able to examine the extent to which each person changed his or her attitudes over the course of the campaign. Importantly, panel data are necessary *but not sufficient* for assessing change over time at the individual level. One must also employ special statistical methods in order to test hypotheses about individual-level change. We rely on fixed-effects regression because it not only provides estimates of individual-level change but also, as we explain later, allows us to make the strongest possible causal inferences outside of an experiment about the impact of exposure to Obama on change in racial attitudes.

Fixed-effects regression assesses within-person change by comparing each respondent to himself or herself at an earlier point in time. A basic fixed-effects model estimates the average amount of over-time change in a dependent variable, as in chapter 2, where we examined change in white racial prejudice during the 2008 presidential campaign. In the model, we include wave variables representing the passage of time (between each pair of panel waves) as predictors of change in racial prejudice. Although fixed-effects models estimate change for each individual respondent, the coefficients for the wave variables present the average amount of change across all respondents. The negative coefficients for the wave variables in our model indicate that white Americans, on average, became less prejudiced against blacks during the campaign.

In chapters 4 and 5, we use more complex fixed-effects models to suggest that mass media exposure to the Obama campaign played an important role in helping to reduce white racial prejudice. Specifically, we argue that increases over time in exposure to Obama via mass media led to reductions in white racial prejudice. For testing this hypothesis, fixed-effects models of within-person change provide a huge improvement over other observational designs, including other panel models.[1] The advantages of this approach for disentangling preexisting individual differences from actual change are tremendous. As noted earlier, with fixed effects each individual is compared to himself or herself at an earlier point in time, and as a result *all* differences *between* individuals drop out of the equation. By contrast, Larry Bartels notes, "in individual-level cross-sectional studies, differences in opinions between those exposed to the media and those who remain unexposed may simply reflect preexisting differences between the two groups in political attitudes or characteristics."[2] Fixed-effects regression discards all between-person variance and uses only within-person variance that occurs over time. Stable factors such as education, income, age, ongoing political interest, and party identification drop out of the model, as do *all* other variables (whether observable or unobservable) that are constant over time.[3] Researchers using cross-sectional designs try to measure and control for the most likely spurious confounders, but this approach does not address all of the other variables that we are unaware of or cannot measure (that is, unobserved heterogeneity bias). This is the single greatest threat to interpreting causal relationships in observational research, and fixed-effects regression solves it.[4]

Moreover, fixed-effects regression does a superior job of controlling for stable confounders compared to traditional panel analyses using lagged dependent variable models (LDVMs) or, by extension, cross-lagged models.[5] Although scholars often refer to LDVMs as if they assess change at the individual level, this is misleading because these models still rely on between-person variance and only assess change in the limited sense of differences over time in the rank-order of individuals. In other words, if all respondents decline, say, in racial prejudice by the same amount, an LDVM would suggest that no change has occurred, which is clearly misleading.[6] Further, owing to measurement error alone, the measure of the lagged dependent variable provides imperfect control for preexisting differences; even after adjusting for measurement error, "the use of the Y1 regressor variable seems to underadjust for prior differences."[7] Fixed-effects regression, on the other hand, *perfectly* controls for preexisting differences by only comparing each individual to himself or herself at an earlier point in time.

In fixed-effects regression, only variables that change over time can produce spurious associations. Fortunately, spuriousness arising from time-varying factors in fixed-effects models is far less likely than spuriousness arising from individual differences in between-person models. In between-person models, a confounding variable merely needs to be correlated with the independent and dependent variables. But with fixed effects, a confounding variable would have to (1) change over time, (2) explain change over time in the independent variable, and (3) explain change over time in the dependent variable. Especially in the relatively short time span of a presidential campaign, very few potential confounders meet these requirements.[8] Moreover, by including a dummy variable for survey wave in each equation, we efficiently capture the average total effects of all other time-varying influences.[9] For example, to the extent that political interest rises across the board during a campaign, the effects of the wave variable capture this change. In sum, for all of the reasons described earlier, fixed-effects regression provides the strongest possible causal tests outside of fully randomized experiments.[10]

In addition to examining the amount of change in racial prejudice in relation to independent variables that also change over time, we used fixed-effects models to investigate whether levels of prejudice changed at different rates among different subgroups of the population (see chapter 2 for details). Individual characteristics such as education, income, and region of residence did not change appreciably during the short time span of the 2008 campaign, and as described earlier, fixed-effects models estimate only the quantities of things that change over time; things that do not change obviously do not cause changes in the dependent variable. Nonetheless, it is possible to test hypotheses about differential change within subgroups of the population by including in our models an interaction between the wave variables, which do change over time, and individual difference variables. The interaction coefficient tells us whether prejudice changed at different rates by varying levels of the individual difference variable, such as by different levels of education.

APPENDIX B

Wording of the Survey Items

THE SURVEY

The National Annenberg Election Study (NAES) panel includes waves 1 through 5, and the Russell Sage Foundation (RSF) Recontact Study includes wave 6.

NUMBER OF POLITICAL TV SHOWS VIEWED
(WAVES 2, 4, 5, AND 6)

On waves 2, 4, and 5, respondents were first asked, "From which of the following sources have you heard anything about the presidential campaign?" and the following choices were listed: television news programs (morning or evening), newspapers, television talk shows, public affairs or news analysis programs, Internet sites, chat rooms or blogs, radio news or radio talk shows, newsmagazines, or "Have not heard anything about the presidential campaign." On wave 6, respondents were asked, "From which of the following sources have you heard anything about politics?"

Respondents who said that they had heard about the campaign from television were then asked, "Which of the following programs do you watch regularly on television? Please check any that you watch at least once a month," followed by a list of programs with checkboxes beside them and a "none of the above" option. Three additional lists of programs were shown at different points in the survey.

For the analyses including waves 2, 4, and 5, we rely on responses to the forty-nine programs that appeared on all three waves: *ABC News: Nightline, ABC World News, Today Show, NBC Nightly News, The NewsHour with Jim Lehrer, BET News, Fox News, Good Morning America, CBS Evening News, CBS Morning News, CNN Headline News/Newsroom, The Tonight Show with Jay Leno, America This Morning, The Daily Show with Jon Stewart, 60 Minutes, The Late Show with David Letterman, The O'Reilly Factor, The Early Show, Ellen DeGeneres Show, Face the Nation, Fox & Friends, Frontline, Hannity & Colmes, Hannity's America, Hardball with Chris Matthews, Late Edition with Wolf Blitzer, Meet the Press, MSNBC Live, Out in the Open, Oprah, Situation Room, Special Report with Brit Hume, Larry King Live, CBS Sunday Morning, The Beltway Boys, 20/20, The Fox Report with Shepard Smith, This Week with George Stephanopoulos, The View, Lou Dobbs, The Colbert Report, Anderson Cooper 360, Geraldo at Large, Countdown with Keith Olbermann, Dateline NBC, Studio B with Shepard Smith, Reliable Sources, Your World with Neil Cavuto,* and *McLaughlin Group.*

For the analyses including waves 5 and 6, we rely on responses to the forty-eight programs that appeared on those two waves: *ABC News: Nightline, ABC World News, Today Show, NBC Nightly News, The NewsHour with Jim Lehrer/ PBS NewsHour, BET News, Fox News, Good Morning America, CBS Evening News, CBS Morning News, CNN Headline News/Newsroom, The Tonight Show with Jay Leno, America This Morning, The Daily Show with Jon Stewart, 60 Minutes, The Late Show with David Letterman, The O'Reilly Factor, The Early Show, Ellen DeGeneres Show, Face the Nation, Fox & Friends, Frontline, Hannity & Colmes/Hannity, Hannity's America, Hardball with Chris Matthews, Meet the Press, MSNBC Live, Oprah, Situation Room, Special Report with Brit Hume/ Special Report with Bret Baier, Larry King Live, CBS Sunday Morning, 20/20, The Fox Report with Shepard Smith, This Week with George Stephanopoulos/ This Week with Christiane Amanpour, The View, The Colbert Report, Anderson Cooper 360, Geraldo at Large, Countdown with Keith Olbermann, Dateline NBC, Studio B with Shepard Smith, Reliable Sources, Your World with Neil Cavuto, McLaughlin Group, America's Election Headquarters/America's News Headquarters, Morning Joe,* and *The Rachel Maddow Show.*

CATEGORIZING TV SHOWS AS CONSERVATIVE, LIBERAL, OR NEUTRAL

We follow Susanna Dilliplane's method of categorization of the television programs as slanted toward liberals, as slanted toward conservatives, or as neutral.[1]

Conservative TV Shows

The Beltway Boys, Fox & Friends, Fox News, The Fox Report with Shepard Smith, Geraldo at Large, Hannity & Colmes, Hannity's America, The O'Reilly Factor, Special Report with Brit Hume, Studio B with Shepard Smith, Your World with Neil Cavuto, America's Election Headquarters, and *Morning Joe.*

Liberal TV Shows

ABC Nightline, Anderson Cooper 360, BET News, CNN Headline News/ Newsroom, The Colbert Report, Countdown with Keith Olbermann, The Daily Show, Good Morning America, Hardball with Chris Matthews, Late Edition with Wolf Blitzer, MSNBC Live, Out in the Open, Situation Room, The View, This Week with George Stephanopoulos, and *The Rachel Maddow Show.*

Neutral TV Shows

ABC World News, America This Morning, CBS Evening News, CBS Morning News, CBS Sunday Morning, Dateline, The Early Show, Face the Nation, Frontline, Larry King Live, Lou Dobbs, McLaughlin Group, Meet the Press, NBC Nightly News, The NewsHour with Jim Lehrer, Reliable Sources, The Today Show, 20/20, and *60 Minutes.*

POLITICAL INTEREST (GFK PROFILE AND WAVES 2 AND 3)

"In general, how interested are you in politics and public affairs?" (very interested, somewhat interested, slightly interested, not at all interested).

SELF-PERCEIVED KNOWLEDGE ABOUT OBAMA (WAVES 1, 2, AND 3)

"How much would you say you know about each of these people? For each name, please tell us whether you know quite a lot, a fair amount, a little, or almost nothing at all about this person." (Showed the name "Barack Obama" along with these four response options.)

WHITE RACIAL PREJUDICE (WAVES 3, 4, 5, 6, AND 7)

Whites rated whites and blacks on three scales—hardworking to lazy, intelligent to unintelligent, and trustworthy to untrustworthy.

"Next are some questions about various groups in our society. Below are left-right scales on which you can rate characteristics of people in different groups. For the first item below, the far left side of the scale means that you think most of the people in that group are extremely 'hardworking.' Placing the slider on the far right side means that you think most of the people in that group are extremely 'lazy.' The middle means that you think the people in this group are not particularly toward one end or the other."

As practice, respondents were first asked, "Where would you rate physicians in general on this scale?" Immediately after, respondents were asked to rate either whites or blacks, and later in the survey they were asked about the other group (with the order randomized). "Where would you rate whites in general on these scales?" "Where would you rate blacks in general on these scales?" Here is an example of one of the scales:

Hard  Lazy
working

PERCEPTIONS OF RACE RELATIONS (WAVES 3, 4, 5, AND 6)
Over three items, respondents were asked for their perceptions of race relations today, over the past ten years, and over the next ten years.

"In general, do you think race relations in the U.S. are . . ." (very bad, fairly bad, neither good nor bad, fairly good, very good).

"Over the course of the past 10 years, do you feel that race relations have . . ." (gotten a lot worse, gotten a little worse, stayed about the same, gotten a little better, gotten a lot better).

"Looking ahead 10 years from today, do you feel that race relations will . . ." (get a lot worse, get a little worse, stay about the same, get a little better, get a lot better).

ECONOMIC PERCEPTIONS (WAVES 3, 4, 5, AND 6)
Respondents were asked two questions:

"We are interested in how people are getting along financially these days. Would you say that you and your family living here are better off, worse off, or just about the same financially as you were a year ago?" (a lot better off, a little better off, a little worse off, a lot worse off, just about the same).

"Thinking about the economy in the country as a whole, would you say that over the past year the nation's economy has gotten better, stayed about the same, or gotten worse?" (gotten a lot better, gotten a little better, gotten a little worse, gotten a lot worse, stayed about the same).

APPENDIX C

Demographics of the Survey Samples of Non-Hispanic Whites

Table A.1   Appendix C: Demographics of the Survey Samples, Non-Hispanic Whites

	U.S. Census (July 2008 CPS)	NAES, Waves 3, 4, and 5 (2008)	RSF, Wave 6 (2010)
Education			
High school or less	40.3%	21.7%	23.3%
Some college	29.3	32.3	31.0
College graduate	19.9	27.3	26.3
Postgraduate work	10.5	18.7	19.4
	(N = 74,315)	(N = 2,636)	(N = 3,263)
Income			
Less than $25,000	16.3%	13.4%	13.0%
$25,000 to 49,999	24.6	26.4	27.9
$50,000 to 74,999	21.6	21.8	22.7
$75,000 to 99,999	14.6	16.6	15.7
$100,000 or more	22.8	21.7	20.7
	(N = 60,790)	(N = 2,636)	(N = 3,263)
Age			
Eighteen to twenty-nine	17.9%	6.0%	7.1%
Thirty to forty-four	24.5	24.0	24.0
Forty-five to fifty-nine	29.9	36.9	37.4
Sixty or older	27.7	33.0	31.5
	(N = 74,315)	(N = 2,636)	(N = 3,263)

(continued)

Table A1   (Continued)

	U.S. Census (July 2008 CPS)	NAES, Waves 3, 4, and 5 (2008)	RSF, Wave 6 (2010)
Gender			
Male	48.3%	47.6%	47.3%
Female	51.7	52.4	52.7
	(N = 74,315)	(N = 2,636)	(N = 3,263)

Source: 2008 CPS; 2008 NAES Panel Survey; 2010 RSF Recontact Study.
Note: Data are unweighted.

APPENDIX D

Details of the Content Analysis

In this appendix, we provide details of our searches of media content that used the large-scale Internet-based Lydia System, and, for testing validity, comparisons to searches of Lexis-Nexis.

COVERAGE OF OBAMA

We used a search of "Barack Obama" for the time period covered by the NAES sample, that is, from July 17, 2008, through January 31, 2009. The search automatically captured different spellings and capitalizations, such as references to "Obama," "Barack Hussein Obama," and the like. The results of the search and a Lexis-Nexis search using the term "Obama" revealed a high degree of correspondence between the two ($r = 0.82$, $p < 0.001$), providing strong evidence of convergent validity.[1]

COVERAGE OF OBAMA MENTIONING RACE

We conducted a search of the number of references to "Barack Obama" and "black" in the same sentence. Although this may seem like a simplistic way to search for all references to Obama and race, the results strongly correlate with a search using numerous additional terms to capture white/black identities in Lexis-Nexis ($r = 0.77$, $p < 0.001$).[2]

To assess the reliability and validity of the Lexis-Nexis search, one of the co-authors hand-coded a random sample of coverage of Obama and then compared the results with those of the Lexis-Nexis search.[3] There was 97 per-cent agreement between our hand-coding of the sample and the Lexis-Nexis search results. Moreover, we found no evidence of Type 1 error: of the daily broadcasts retrieved by the Lexis-Nexis search (forty-eight), all were coded as mentioning race. And we found only minimal evidence of Type 2 error: of the daily broadcasts coded as mentioning race (fifty-one), the Lexis-Nexis search retrieved most of them (forty-eight).

COVERAGE MENTIONING RACISM

We first created a Boolean search term in Lexis-Nexis, from which we drew terms for the search using the larger database of U.S. news sources. To test the reliability and validity of the Lexis-Nexis search term, we randomly sampled from the Lexis-Nexis results for the search of coverage of Obama mention-ing race and then compared one co-author's hand-coding of the sample with the automated Lexis-Nexis results. That comparison revealed high reliability (89 percent agreement) and validity (Type 1 error rate = 10 percent; Type 2 error rate = 16 percent).

Our search in the larger database included "Barack Obama" and one or more of thirteen words/phrases from the Lexis-Nexis search: "bigotry," "Bradley effect," "fear bomb," "fear card," "fear-mongering," "prejudice," "race-baiting," "race card," "racial division," "racial stereotypes," "racial stereotyping," "rac-ism," and "racist."[4] The results of the search were highly correlated with the results of the Lexis-Nexis search ($r = 0.67$, $p < 0.001$).

COVERAGE MENTIONING RACIAL UNITY

As with the previous type of coverage, we first created a Boolean search term in Lexis-Nexis. It quickly became clear, however, that extremely little coverage of Obama mentioned racial unity, making it implausible as an explanation for the decline in racial prejudice; thus, we did not carry out explicit reli-ability and validity tests or conduct additional searches in the larger database. Although there were several high-profile cases where racial unity rhetoric gar-nered substantial coverage, of more than 9,000 Lexis-Nexis hits mentioning Obama, only 109 mentioned racial unity.

It is possible that we found so little coverage of racial unity because our con-ceptualization or measurement was too narrow. One might argue that more general references to unity as Americans, without referencing race explicitly, might have nonetheless promoted racial unity, albeit implicitly. However, the theory and evidence underlying the common in-group identity model strongly suggest that both the in-group and out-group must be explicitly linked to the superordinate category. Thus, we only considered coverage linking whites and blacks to a shared American identity as coverage mentioning racial unity.

THE LEXIS-NEXIS SEARCH TERMS

Coverage of Obama

BODY(obama) *and* SHOW(america's election headquarters *or* anderson cooper 360 *or* beltway boys *or* cbs evening news *or* cbs sunday morning *or* cnn election center *or* countdown *or* dateline NBC *or* early show *or* face the nation *or* good morning america *or* hannity's america *or* hannity colmes *or* hardball *or* larry king live *or* late edition with wolf blitzer *or* lou dobbs tonight *or* mclaughlin group *or* meet the press *or* newshour with jim lehrer *or* nightline *or* nightly news *or* o'reilly factor *or* reliable sources *or* situation room *or* 60 minutes *or* special report with brit hume *or* this week *or* today show *or* 20/20 *or* world news *or* your world with neil cavuto)

Coverage of Obama Mentioning Race

BODY(obama) *and* SHOW(america's election headquarters *or* anderson cooper 360 *or* beltway boys *or* cbs evening news *or* cbs sunday morning *or* cnn election center *or* countdown *or* dateline NBC *or* early show *or* face the nation *or* good morning america *or* hannity's america *or* hannity colmes *or* hardball *or* larry king live *or* late edition with wolf blitzer *or* lou dobbs tonight *or* mclaughlin group *or* meet the press *or* newshour with jim lehrer *or* nightline *or* nightly news *or* o'reilly factor *or* reliable sources *or* situation room *or* 60 minutes *or* special report with brit hume *or* this week *or* today show *or* 20/20 *or* world news *or* your world with neil cavuto) *and* BODY(abolition *or* abolitionist *or* African American *or* anti-black *or* anti-white *or* biracial *or* black American *or* black athlete *or* black audience *or* black candidate *or* black children *or* black church *or* black community *or* black electorate *or* black guy *or* black leader *or* black male *or* black man *or* black men *or* black militant *or* black panther *or* black people *or* black person *or* black population *or* black president *or* black race hustlers *or* black radio *or* black responsibility *or* black society *or* black vote *or* black voter *or* black women *or* blue collar whites *or* civil rights icon *or* civil rights leader *or* civil rights movement *or* civil rights struggle *or* color blind *or* color of his skin *or* color of their skin *or* first black *or* Ku Klux *or* KKK *or* man of color *or* middle class whites *or* negro *or* obama's race *or* people of color *or* person of color *or* post racial *or* race baiting *or* race based *or* race card *or* race issue *or* race relations *or* racial *or* racially *or* racialized *or* racism *or* racist *or* skin color *or* slave *or* slavery *or* struggle for civil rights *or* students of color *or* white blue collar *or* white female voters *or* white guy *or* white independents *or* white kids *or* white male *or* white man *or* white people *or* white pilots *or* white politician *or* white supremacist *or* white vote *or* white voter *or* white women *or* white working class *or* working class white)

Coverage Mentioning Racism

BODY(obama) *and* SHOW(america's election headquarters *or* anderson cooper 360 *or* beltway boys *or* cbs evening news *or* cbs sunday morning *or* cnn election center *or* countdown *or* dateline NBC *or* early show *or* face the nation *or* good morning america *or* hannity's america *or* hannity colmes *or* hardball *or* larry king live *or* late edition with wolf blitzer *or* lou dobbs tonight *or* mclaughlin group *or* meet the press *or* newshour with jim lehrer *or* nightline *or* nightly news *or* o'reilly factor *or* reliable sources *or* situation room *or* 60 minutes *or* special report with brit hume *or* this week *or* today show *or* 20/20 *or* world news *or* your world with neil cavuto) *and* BODY(racist! *or* anti-black *or* bigot! *or* bradley effect *or* fear bomb *or* fear card *or* fear mongering *or* funny name *or* prejudice *or* race baiting *or* race card *or* racial bias *or* racial charge *or* racial division *or* racial epithet *or* racial factor *or* racial fear *or* racial hatred *or* racial innuendo *or* racial resentment *or* racial slur *or* racial stereotype! *or* racial subtext *or* racial! tinge! *or* racial undertone *or* racially divisive *or* racially insensitive *or* sowing seeds of hate!)

Coverage Mentioning Racial Unity

BODY(obama) *and* SHOW(america's election headquarters *or* anderson cooper 360 *or* beltway boys *or* cbs evening news *or* cbs sunday morning *or* cnn election center *or* countdown *or* dateline NBC *or* early show *or* face the nation *or* good morning america *or* hannity's america *or* hannity colmes *or* hardball *or* larry king live *or* late edition with wolf blitzer *or* lou dobbs tonight *or* mclaughlin group *or* meet the press *or* newshour with jim lehrer *or* nightline *or* nightly news *or* o'reilly factor *or* reliable sources *or* situation room *or* 60 minutes *or* special report with brit hume *or* this week *or* today show *or* 20/20 *or* world news *or* your world with neil cavuto) *and* BODY (("all races of our society" *or* "Americans across racial lines" *or* "Americans of all creeds" *or* "Americans of all races" *or* "Americans of every race" *or* "child of every race" *or* "children of every race" *or* "every single creed" *or* "every single race" *or* "people of all colors" *or* "people of all creeds" *or* "people of every creed" *or* "reporters of every race" *or* "women of all races") *or* (African American w/s all Americans) *or* (all races w/s coming together) *or* (black community w/s same issues) *or* (common humanity w/s segregation) *or* (girls w/s all races) *or* (people w/s all races) *or* (racial division w/s common) *or* (religion w/s region w/s young w/s old) *or* (race issues w/s come together) *or* (wall w/s between race) *or* (white w/s all American w/s black) *or* (white w/s all Americans w/s black w/s Hispanic w/s young) *or* (white w/s all kids w/s black w/s Hispanic) *or* (white w/s American w/s asian w/s black) *or* (white w/s American w/s black w/s democrat w/s republican) *or* (white w/s asian w/s black w/s chinese) *or* (white w/s asian w/s black w/s disabled w/s gay) *or* (white w/s asian w/s black w/s Hispanic) *or* (white w/s asian w/s black w/s latino) *or* (white w/s asian w/s black w/s Spanish-speaking) *or* (white w/s black w/s conservative w/s democrat w/s republican) *or* (white w/s black w/s democrat w/s gay w/s republican) *or* (white w/s black w/s democrat w/s republican w/s rich))

NOTES

CHAPTER 1

1. Rachel L. Swarns, "Blacks Debate Civil Rights Risk in Obama's Rise," *New York Times,* August 25, 2008.
2. Remnick (2010), 553.
3. NBC News, November 4, 2008.
4. Randall Kennedy, "The Big 'What If'; The Hopes of Black America Ride on His Shoulders, but the Outcome's Way Up in the Air," *Washington Post,* September 14, 2008.
5. Tesler and Sears (2010).
6. Kinder and Dale-Riddle (2012); see also Pasek et al. (2009).
7. Hollinger (2011), 174.
8. Ibid., 177.
9. See, for example, Schuman et al. (1997).
10. See, for example, Kinder and Kam (2009).
11. See, for example, Bobo et al. (2012), Hutchings (2009), and Kam and Kinder (2007).
12. Adorno et al. (1950).
13. See Bobo and Kluegel (1993).
14. Welch and Sigelman (2011).
15. Of two other surveys conducted during the campaign, one suggested a decline in prejudice (Plant et al. 2009), while the other did not (Schmidt and Nosek 2010), but both surveys relied on unrepresentative samples of whites.
16. Welch and Sigelman (2011), 211.
17. Bodenhausen et al. (1995).

18. Paluck and Green (2009), 343.
19. Hajnal (2001, 2007).
20. Hajnal (2001), 604.
21. See, for example, Kinder and Sanders (1996).
22. See Goldman (2012) and Zillmann and Brosius (2000).
23. See, for example, Entman and Rojecki (2000).
24. For a review, see Pettigrew and Tropp (2011).
25. See, for example, Stephan and Stephan (1985).
26. Plant and Devine (2003).
27. See, for example, Wright et al. (1997).
28. Turner, Crisp, and Lambert (2007).
29. Remnick (2010), 494.
30. For details, see appendix A ("Benefits of Fixed-Effects Regression in Panel Analyses").
31. Allison (2009).
32. Allison (1990, 2009) and Halaby (2004).
33. Allison (1990, 2009) and Achen (2000).
34. Halaby (2004).
35. Allison (2009).

CHAPTER 2

1. Huddy and Feldman (2009).
2. See, for example, Schuman et al. (1997).
3. Kinder and Sanders (1996), 93.
4. Kinder and Sears (1981), 416.
5. Sniderman et al. (1991), 424.
6. Kinder and Sanders (1996), 106.
7. See, for example, Henry and Sears (2002), Kinder and Mendelberg (2000), Rabinowitz et al. (2009), and Tarman and Sears (2005).
8. Feldman and Huddy (2005).
9. Ibid.
10. For further evidence, see ibid.
11. Greenwald and Banaji (1995).
12. Blanton and Jaccard (2008), 278.
13. Greenwald, McGhee, and Schwartz (1998).
14. Arkes and Tetlock (2004), 260.
15. Payne et al. (2005).

16. Arkes and Tetlock (2004), 262.
17. Another critique of the IAT is that rather than implicit associations demonstrating prejudice against blacks, such associations might indicate other negative emotions like pity, anxiety, embarrassment, sorrow, frustration, or guilt (Arkes and Tetlock 2004; see also Olson and Fazio 2004).
18. Kalmoe and Piston (2013); compare to Pasek et al. (2009).
19. Greenwald et al. (2009) and Payne et al. (2010).
20. Adorno et al. (1950).
21. Kinder and Kam (2009). See also, for example, Bobo and Kluegel (1993).
22. See, for example, Bobo and Kluegel (1993, 1997), Carmines, Sniderman, and Easter (2011), Hutchings (2009), Kinder and Kam (2009), Kinder and Sanders (1996), and Piston (2010).
23. Brewer (1999).
24. "Following," Piston adds, "McCauley et al. (1980) and Kinder and Mendelberg (1995)" (Piston 2010, 436, emphasis in the original).
25. For the question wording of the items, see appendix B ("Wording of the Survey Items").
26. Cronbach's alphas for waves 3, 4, and 5 are 0.90, 0.90, and 0.91, respectively (N = 2,636).
27. Heise (1969). The true-score reliability using the Heise (1969) method for panel data is 0.75. Unlike reliability assessments such as Cronbach's alpha, true-score reliabilities separate measurement error from change in underlying true-scores, thus providing a measure of reliability that is *independent* of stability (for further discussion, see Dilliplane, Goldman, and Mutz 2013). True-score reliabilities are rarely calculated because this assessment requires three or more waves of panel data. Indeed, to our knowledge, no prior study has assessed the true-score reliability of this measure of racial prejudice.
28. Ninety-five percent of wave 3 respondents had values ranging from 0 to 40 (mean = 8.16, standard deviation = 15.01, N = 2,636); 95 percent of wave 4 respondents had values ranging from 0 to 35 (mean = 7.10, standard deviation = 14.57, N = 2,636); and 95 percent of wave 5 respondents had values ranging from 0 to 33 (mean = 6.09, standard deviation = 13.20, N = 2,636).
29. Among the panel sample of whites (N = 2,636), one-quarter to one-third evaluated blacks more favorably than whites on any given wave, but most of those people had differences that were very close to 0; the distribution on the negative end was highly skewed. In any case, using the difference scores without recoding the negative values to 0 does not change our main findings.

30. Kinder and Kam (2009), 44.

31. Ibid., 46–47.

32. On face-to-face and telephone surveys, see, for example, Kinder and Sanders (1996) and Kuklinski, Cobb, and Gilens (1997).

33. Asking whites about their own in-group first produced *less* positive attitudes toward blacks relative to whites asked about their in-group second (wave 3: mean = 6.75 and mean = 12.43, $p < 0.001$; wave 4: mean = 9.75 and mean = 13.98, $p < 0.001$; wave 5: mean = 9.89 and mean = 12.75, $p < 0.001$; N = 2,636). And asking whites about blacks first produced *more* positive attitudes toward their own in-group relative to whites asked about blacks second (wave 3: mean = 14.62 and mean = 17.79, $p < 0.001$; wave 4: mean = 16.33 and mean = 19.14, $p < 0.001$; wave 5: mean = 14.67 and mean = 17.56, $p < 0.001$; N = 2,636).

34. See, for example, Kuklinski and Cobb (1998, 46); see also Jackman (1978, 1981), Jackman and Muha (1984), and Krysan (1998).

35. Demonstrating that racial prejudice declined more among the lower-educated, a fixed-effects analysis of within-person change revealed a significant positive interaction between education (in years) and the wave 5 dummy variable (0.22, $p < 0.05$). Note that this is unlikely to be due to a floor effect, as the higher-educated exhibited a substantial amount of prejudice in all three survey waves.

36. The 2008 NAES data were collected by GfK (formerly Knowledge Networks), which recruits large nationally representative samples. GfK maintains a large panel of respondents from which the NAES sample was drawn.

37. Kalmoe and Piston (2013); compare to Pasek et al. (2009).

38. Columb and Plant (2011).

39. Kinder and Sanders (1996).

40. Valentino and Brader (2011).

41. Confusion may arise because Valentino and Brader (2011) report that racial resentment increased among the one-third of their sample who also perceived less discrimination against blacks after the election. However, both studies' findings suggest decreased prejudice in the sample as a whole.

42. Bobo and Kluegel (1993), 454.

43. Kinder and Kam (2009), Kam and Kinder (2007, 2012), Kinder and Drake (2009), and Kinder and Dale-Riddle (2012).

44. See, for example, Federico (2004), Federico and Sidanius (2002), Feldman and Huddy (2005), Hurtwitz and Peffley (1997, 2005), and Hutchings (2009).

45. For details, see appendix C ("Demographics of the Survey Samples").

46. Allison (2009).
47. For further explanation of fixed-effects regression, see appendix A ("Benefits of Fixed-Effects Regression in Panel Analyses").
48. Because fixed-effects panel models focus specifically on within-person variance, the main effects of individual differences drop out of these models because stable independent variables do not predict change over time in the dependent variable. Nonetheless, it is still possible to examine whether certain groups changed more over time than others by including interactions between those unchanging characteristics and the wave variables. This approach allows us to assess differential change over time by population subgroups.
49. Schuman et al. (1997).
50. Kinder and Dale-Riddle (2012), Kinder and Drake (2009), and Welch and Sigelman (2011).
51. Unfortunately, the ANES and GSS have included the racial prejudice items that we used only since the early 1990s, thus precluding comparison to major periods of change in racial prejudice that may have occurred during the preceding decades.

CHAPTER 3

1. Marc Fisher, "Rapture in the Streets as Multitudes Cheer Obama and Celebrate America," *Washington Post,* November 6, 2008.
2. Alice Gomstyn, "Obama as a Role Model: Students, Educators Share Excitement," *ABC News,* November 5, 2008, available at: http://abcnews. go.com/US/story?id=6184328&page=1; Byron Pitts, "'Obama Effect' Touching a New Generation," *CBS News,* August 26, 2008, available at: http:// www.cbsnews.com/stories/2008/08/26/eveningnews/main4386451.shtml; and Jahshua Smith, "Obama, Role Model for All," *The State News,* June 17, 2009, available at: http://www.statenews.com/index.php/article/2008/06/obama_ role_model_for_all_.
3. See, for example, Laura Meckler, "Obama, Stimulus Proposals Enjoy Broad Backing in Poll," *Wall Street Journal,* January 15, 2009; and Sheryl Gay Stolberg and Marjorie Connelly, "Obama Nudging Views on Race, a Survey Finds," *New York Times,* April 28, 2009.
4. Hollinger (2011), 174.
5. Bob Herbert, "Take a Bow, America," *New York Times,* November 8, 2008.

6. See Fields and Fields (2012).

7. Jesse Washington, "Obama's Candidacy Sparks Race Dialogue," Associated Press, September 28, 2008.

8. Susan Page, "Hopes for Race Relations Are High," *USA Today,* July 14, 2008.

9. Valentino and Brader (2011).

10. Valentino and Brader (2011) find this pattern for immigration policies, but not for attitudes toward the death penalty. We do not include these in our discussion because neither issue area is even remotely considered a policy designed to redress the effects of racial discrimination, so it is unclear why improvements in race relations should change people's attitudes toward these issues.

11. Ibid., 218.

12. Jhally and Lewis (1992).

13. Ibid.

14. Bodenhausen et al. (1995).

15. Valentino and Brader (2011).

16. See, for example, Welch and Sigelman (2011).

17. Frank Newport, "Americans See Obama Election as Race Relations Milestone," Gallup Politics, November 7, 2008, available at: http://www.gallup.com/poll/111817/Americans-See-Obama-Election-Race-Relations-Milestone.aspx.

18. See, for example, Tesler and Sears (2010) and Ansolabehere and Stewart (2009). Stephen Ansolabehere and Charles Stewart, whose analysis rests on treating blacks and Hispanics as a single group, note that if both groups had voted Democratic in 2008 at the same rates as in 2004, McCain would have won.

19. Tesler and Sears (2010), 7.

20. See Sniderman and Stiglitz (2008) and Tesler and Sears (2010).

21. Jackson (2008a).

22. Jackson (2008b).

23. Sarah Kershaw, "Talk About Race? Relax, It's O.K." *New York Times,* January 14, 2009.

24. Plant and Devine (2003).

25. See, for example, Stephan and Stephan (1985).

26. Steele (2010).

27. Marx, Ko, and Friedman (2009).

28. Aronson et al. (2009).

29. Brody et al. (2006), Cassisi et al. (2006), and James et al. (1987).

30. Paradies (2006) and Williams and Mohammed (2009).

31. Pieterse et al. (2012).

32. See, for example, Kaiser et al. (2009).

CHAPTER 4

1. Paluck and Green (2009), 343.

2. Remnick (2010), 494.

3. See, for example, Entman and Rojecki (2000) and Dixon (2008).

4. Allport (1954).

5. See, for example, ibid. and Amir (1969).

6. Pettigrew (1998).

7. Pettigrew and Tropp (2006).

8. Pettigrew and Tropp (2011).

9. Zajonc (1968).

10. Pettigrew and Tropp (2011).

11. Zebrowitz, White, and Wieneke (2008).

12. Pettigrew and Tropp (2011), 64.

13. Charles (2003) and Logan (2001).

14. Smith (2002).

15. Dixon and Rosenbaum (2004).

16. Stephan and Stephan (1985).

17. Plant and Devine (2003).

18. See, for example, Stephan and Stephan (1985).

19. Paolini et al. (2004) and Wright et al. (1997).

20. Wright et al. (1997).

21. Turner et al. (2007).

22. Zebrowitz et al. (2008).

23. Reeves and Nass (1996).

24. Grabe et al. (1999), Lombard et al. (2000), and Reeves et al. (1999).

25. For a review, see Mutz and Goldman (2010).

26. See, for example, Dixon (2008), Gross (1984), Lee, Farrell, and Link (2004), and Vidmar and Rokeach (1974).

27. For example, Gross (1984), Oppliger (2007), and Signorielli (1989).

28. See, for example Ball-Rokeach, Grube, and Rokeach (1981); see also Morgan (1982, 1987).

29. For example, Rossler and Brosius (2001) and Schiappa, Greg, and Hewes (2005).

30. Ford (1997).

31. Power, Murphy, and Coover (1996).

32. Smith and Zarate (1992).

33. Schwarz and Bless (1992b).

34. Schwarz and Bless (1992a).

35. Bodenhausen et al. (1995).

36. Dasgupta and Greenwald (2001); see also Mitchell, Nosek, and Banaji (2003). With regard to Colin Powell, Donald Kinder and Corrine McConnaughy have argued that "Powell's popularity does nothing to induce whites to rethink their stereotypes." However, their survey analyses did not examine whether exposure to Powell influenced levels of racial prejudice; instead, they assessed the cross-sectional predictors of Powell's (and other black leaders') popularity. Kinder and McConnaughy (2006), 163.

37. Wittenbrink, Judd, and Park (2001).

38. Barden et al. (2004).

39. See, for example, Ramasubramanian (2011) and Zillmann and Brosius (2000).

40. Morgan (1982), Rossler and Brosius (2001), Schiappa et al. (2005), and Zillmann and Brosius (2000).

41. Columb and Plant (2011).

42. Welch and Sigelman (2011).

43. Although three other surveys were carried out as the 2008 campaign unfolded, they all used unrepresentative convenience samples; see Bernstein, Young, and Claypool (2010), Plant et al. (2009), and Schmidt and Nosek (2010).

44. A complete list of the programs can be found in appendix B ("Wording of the Survey Items").

45. On programs other than network news programs, see Williams and Delli Carpini (2011).

46. Dilliplane, Goldman, and Mutz (2012) and Goldman, Mutz, and Dilliplane (2013).

47. See, for example, Huber and Arceneaux (2007).

48. For further explanation, see appendix A ("Benefits of Fixed-Effects Regression in Panel Analyses").

49. Halaby (2004).

50. Allison (2009).

51. Ibid., 3.

52. For further explanation, see appendix A ("Benefits of Fixed-Effects Regression in Panel Analyses").

53. Although fixed-effects regression controls for the *constant* effects of all individual characteristics, the impact of those characteristics could *vary* over time. We

replicated all of the analyses including interactions between the wave variables and education, age, gender, income, ideology, party identification, and political interest. This did not appreciably change the size of the exposure coefficients or their p-values.

54.   See, for example, Sniderman, Hagendoorn, and Prior (2004).

55.   One might point to interpersonal discussion as another alternative explanation. Yet the two-step flow of communication posits that a small number of "opinion leaders" watch political television and then spread the message to many other people; see Katz and Lazarsfeld (1955). In other words, interpersonal influence is a potential mediator of media influence, not a spurious confounder.

56.   State-by-state estimates of television advertising spending during the 2008 campaign can be found at "ElectionCenter2008: Election Tracker: Ad Spending," CNNPolitics.com, available at: www.cnn.com/election/2008/map/ad.spending.

57.   The average amount of spending in the top twenty-five states was $10.93 million, whereas the average amount of spending in the bottom twenty-five states was a mere $224,000. We find the same pattern of results comparing states with $10 million (or $15 million) in television advertising by the Obama campaign to states with less than $1 million in advertising. Likewise, we get the same results when comparing states classified as "battleground" versus "nonbattleground" by news media organizations such as The Cook Political Report and the *Washington Post*.

58.   Bodenhausen et al. (1995).

59.   Fiske (1980) and Skowronski and Carlston (1987, 1989).

60.   Maoz (2003), Page-Gould, Mendoza-Denton, and Tropp (2008), and Pettigrew and Tropp (2006).

61.   Dilliplane (2011). For the list of programs by category, see appendix B ("Wording of the Survey Items").

62.   See, for example, Cooper and Jahoda (1947) and Kendall and Wolf (1949).

63.   Brown and Hewstone (2005) and Brewer, Dull, and Lui (1981).

64.   Rothbart and John (1985).

65.   Allport (1954), 23.

66.   Pettigrew and Tropp (2011).

67.   Bodenhausen et al. (1995), Gurwitz and Dodge (1977), and Weber and Crocker (1983).

68. Paluck (2009).

69. Vidmar and Rokeach (1974).

CHAPTER 5

1. We focus on coverage about *ongoing* rather than *past* racism because coverage of historical injustices is likely to be interpreted by prejudiced whites as evidence that racism is no longer a problem and thus self-reflection about one's own racial attitudes is unnecessary.

2. "Racism Without the Racists," *Seattle Post-Intelligencer,* October 8, 2008.

3. Kalmoe and Piston (2013).

4. Emily Bazelon and John Dickerson, "Why Is Obama Our First Black President?" *Slate,* November 21, 2008.

5. "Road to Racial Tolerance Is Paved, but Potholes Persist," *Dallas Morning News,* January 19, 2008.

6. "Election Spurs 'Hundreds' of Race Threats, Crimes," Associated Press, November 16, 2008.

7. Kevin Merida, "Racist Incidents Give Some Obama Campaigners Pause," *Washington Post,* May 13, 2008.

8. Monteith et al. (2002).

9. Lowery, Hardin, and Sinclair (2001).

10. Blanchard et al. (1991), Blanchard et al. (1994), and Monteith, Deneen, and Tooman (1996).

11. Macrae, Bodenhausen, and Milne (1998).

12. Ibid. and Macrae et al. (1994).

13. See, for example, Monteith, Sherman, and Devine (1998).

14. Wyer, Sherman, and Stroessner (2000); see also Monteith, Spicer, and Tooman (1998).

15. Kevin Merida, "Racist Incidents Give Some Obama Campaigners Pause," *Washington Post,* May 13, 2008.

16. For the common in-group identity model, see Gaertner and Dovidio (2000).

17. Kinder and Kam (2009).

18. See Gaertner and Dovidio (2005).

19. See, for example, Gaertner et al. (1989) and Nier et al. (2001).

20. Banker and Gaertner (1998), Gaertner et al. (1994), and Gaertner, Dovidio, and Bachman (1996).

21. Dovidio et al. (1997), Gaertner et al. (1990), and Gonzalez and Brown (2003).

22. Gaertner et al. (1990).

23. Transue (2007).
24. Richardson (2005).
25. Mendelberg (2001).
26. Brown and Hewstone (2005).
27. Ensari and Miller (2002).
28. Miller (2002).
29. Brewer and Miller (1984).
30. See Bautin et al. (2010), Lloyd, Kechagias, and Skiena (2005), and Key et al. (2010).
31. Kenski, Hardy, and Jamieson (2010).
32. For instance, a search of CNN's *The Situation Room* typically returns "hits" of more than seven thousand words each, while the same search of ABC's *Good Morning America* typically returns hits of less than one hundred words each.
33. Adding the interaction to the model in column 2 did reduce the size of the coefficient for the number of political TV shows viewed relative to the model in column 1, but still significantly increased the explanatory power of the model. Although the within-person R-squared coefficient is unsurprisingly small in all of the models, given the much greater difficulty of explaining within-person rather than between-person variance, adding the interaction increased its size by about 6 percent (from 0.036 to 0.038)—a statistically significant improvement ($p < 0.05$).

    Within this context, the reduced size of the coefficient for the number of political TV shows viewed has substantive implications, rather than just indicating collinearity. From the standpoint of the underlying theory, change in the number of political TV shows viewed should produce change in racial prejudice *especially when* accompanied by change in the amount of coverage of Obama. Hence, after taking account of the interaction between these two variables, change in the number of political TV shows viewed should have a much smaller effect. In other words, the effect of change in the number of political TV shows viewed ought to matter *less* among those for whom coverage of Obama did not change, compared to those for whom coverage of Obama did change.
34. Mutz and Goldman (2010).
35. Columb and Plant (2011).
36. For instance, one suggestion is that coverage of Obama reduced prejudice not because Obama countered racial stereotypes but rather because coverage showed whites supporting him. This is a plausible hypothesis in light of research on the extended contact hypothesis, which has shown that simply knowing that an in-group member is friends with an out-group member can reduce out-group prejudice (Wright et al. 1997). However, it is unclear how this account can explain the

particularly strong Obama effect among conservatives and those viewing conservative political television (Goldman 2012); these cases involved seeing (fellow conservative) whites opposing Obama more than supporting him.

CHAPTER 6

1. Zillmann and Brosius (2000), 111.
2. Ibid.
3. Gilens (2000).
4. The total sample size for the wave 6 panel of whites is 3,263. Wave 6 was fielded between September 21 and October 6, 2010.
5. Baum and Kernell (1999).
6. Ibid.
7. Pew Research Center (2010).
8. Ibid.
9. Dixon (2008), 322.
10. See, for example, Sears and Kinder (1985).
11. The wave 6 recontact study of African Americans was fielded between October 14 and November 9, 2010. The vast majority (78.5 percent) of those invited to participate completed the survey, producing a total sample size of 756.
12. Druckman, Fein, and Leeper (2012).

CHAPTER 7

1. See Paluck and Green (2009), 343.
2. Devine (1989) and Fazio et al. (1995).
3. See Hamilton (1981) and Macrae, Hewstone, and Griffith (1993).
4. Hajnal (2001), 604; see also Macrae et al. (1993) and Weber and Crocker (1983).
5. Glaser and Ryan (2013), 150.
6. Hajnal (2001).
7. Rachel L. Swarns. "Blacks Debate Civil Rights Risk in Obama's Rise," *New York Times*, August 25, 2008.
8. Bobo et al. (2012).
9. See, for example, Coates (2012).
10. See, for example, Henry Louis Gates Jr., "TV's Black World Turns—But Stays Unreal," *New York Times*, November 12, 1989.
11. See, for example, Gilens (2000).
12. Tim Arango, "Before Obama, There Was Bill Cosby," *New York Times*, November 7, 2008.

13. Jhally and Lewis (1992).
14. Bodenhausen et al. (1995).
15. Bobo et al. (2012).
16. Bodenhausen et al. (1995), 52.
17. Ramasubramanian (2011).
18. Byron Pitts. " 'Obama Effect' Touching a New Generation," *CBS News Online*, August 26, 2008. Available at: http://www.cbsnews.com/news/obama-effect-touching-a-new-generation (accessed February 22, 2014).
19. Kevin Merida. "Racist Incidents Give Some Obama Campaigners Pause," *Washington Post*, May 14, 2008.
20. Richard Wolffe, "Across the Divide: How Barack Obama Is Shaking Up Old Assumptions About What It Means to Be Black and White in America," *Newsweek*, July 15, 2007.
21. Shelby Steele, "Obama's Post-Racial Promise," *Los Angeles Times*, November 5, 2008.
22. Remnick (2010), 551.
23. See, for example, Huddy and Feldman (2009) and Sniderman and Stiglitz (2008).
24. See, for example, Arkes and Tetlock (2004).
25. Allport (1954).
26. Paluck (2009).
27. Charles (2003, 2006).
28. Bobo and Kluegel (1993), Tuch and Hughes (1996), and Wilson (2006).
29. Peffley, Hurwitz, and Sniderman (1997).
30. Jackman (1994).
31. Hutchings (2009), Kinder and Kam (2009), and Kinder and Sanders (1996).
32. Cooper and Jahoda (1947) and Kendall and Wolf (1949).
33. For an exception, see Zaller (1996).
34. Green and Seher (2003), 512.
35. Bartels (1993), 267.
36. On exposure to successful female exemplars, see Dasgupta and Asgari (2004); on mediated contact with positive gay exemplars, see Schiappa et al. (2005).

APPENDIX A

1. Allison (2009).
2. Bartels (1993), 267.
3. More specifically, fixed-effects regression controls for the *constant* effects of individual characteristics, so we also controlled for the time-varying impact of

individual characteristics by including interactions between the wave variables and education, age, gender, income, ideology, party identification, and political interest.

4. Allison (2009) and Halaby (2004).

5. England, Allison, and Wu (2007), 1245; Halaby (2004).

6. For other examples, see Allison (1990).

7. Ibid., 99.

8. See chapter 4 for an in-depth discussion of potential confounders.

9. Halaby (2004).

10. Allison (2009).

APPENDIX B

1. Dilliplane (2011).

APPENDIX D

1. When assessing the correlation between the Lexis-Nexis and Lydia search results, we excluded weekends because television coverage drops cyclically each week on Saturday and Sunday, whereas the same does not happen with newspapers. (If anything, there is an increase in newspaper reading on Sundays.)

2. A search of "Barack Obama" and "African American" had a lower correlation with the Lexis-Nexis results ($r = 0.61$, $p < 0.001$). We also considered the possibility that coverage of Obama may have mentioned race, but just not in the same sentence as his name; thus, we also tried separate searches of "black" and "African American," neither of which correlated very highly with the Lexis-Nexis search. Ultimately, we relied on the search of "Barack Obama" and "black" because it demonstrated the strongest convergent validity with the Lexis-Nexis results.

3. Stryker et al. (2006).

4. The vast majority of coverage mentioning racism during the campaign also mentioned Obama; the daily number of Lexis-Nexis hits for coverage mentioning racism and Obama was almost perfectly correlated with coverage mentioning racism with or without Obama ($r = 0.95$, $p < 0.01$).

   Although the Lydia System database does not allow for Boolean searches that include multiple "and"/"or" propositions, we were able to achieve a similar result by combining the results of several separate searches. We conducted thirteen searches, with each search pairing "Barack Obama" and one of the words/phrases designed to capture coverage mentioning racism. Unfortunately, we could not include more than these thirteen words/phrases from the Lexis-Nexis search because our Lydia searches could only include proper nouns and a limited number of words/phrases designated before the campaign based on the expectation that they would appear in campaign coverage.

REFERENCES

Achen, Chris H. 2000. "Why Lagged Dependent Variables Can Suppress the Explanatory Power of Other Independent Variables." Paper presented to the annual meeting of the Political Methodology Section of the American Political Science Association. Los Angeles, Calif. (July 20–22).

Adorno, Theodor W., Else Frenkel-Brunswik, Daniel J. Levinson, and R. Nevitt Sanford. 1950. *The Authoritarian Personality.* New York: Harper & Row.

Allison, Paul D. 1990. "Change Scores as Dependent Variables in Regression Analysis." In *Sociological Methodology,* edited by Clifford Clogg. Oxford: Basil Blackwell.

———. 2009. *Fixed Effects Regression Models.* Thousand Oaks, Calif.: Sage Publications.

Allport, Gordon W. 1954. *The Nature of Prejudice.* Reading, Mass.: Addison-Wesley.

Amir, Yehuda. 1969. "Contact Hypothesis in Ethnic Relations." *Psychological Bulletin* 71(5): 319–42.

Ansolabehere, Stephen, and Charles Stewart III. 2009. "Amazing Race: How Post-Racial was Obama's Victory?" *Boston Review* (January–February).

Arkes, Hal R., and Philip E. Tetlock. 2004. "Attributions of Implicit Prejudice, or Would Jesse Jackson Fail the Implicit Association Test?" *Psychological Inquiry* 15(4): 257–78.

Aronson, Joshua, Sheana Jannone, Matthew McGlone, and Tanisha Johnson-Campbell. 2009. "The Obama Effect: An Experimental Test." *Journal of Experimental Social Psychology* 45(4): 957–60.

Ball-Rokeach, Sandra J., Joel W. Grube, and Milton Rokeach. 1981. " 'Roots: The Next Generation'—Who Watched and with What Effect?" *Public Opinion Quarterly* 45(1): 58–68.

Banker, Brenda S., and Samuel L. Gaertner. 1998. "Achieving Stepfamily Harmony: An Intergroup-Relations Approach." *Journal of Family Psychology* 12(3): 310–25.

Barden, Jamie, William W. Maddux, Richard E. Petty, and Marilynn B. Brewer. 2004. "Contextual Moderation of Implicit Racial Bias: The Impact of Social Roles on Controlled and Automatically Activated Attitudes." *Journal of Personality and Social Psychology* 87(1): 5–22.

Bartels, Larry M. 1993. "Messages Received: The Political Impact of Media Exposure." *American Political Science Review* 87(2): 267–85.

Baum, Matthew A., and Samuel Kernell. 1999. "Has Cable Ended the Golden Age of Presidential Television?" *American Political Science Review* 93(1): 99–114.

Bautin, Mikhail, Charles B. Ward, Akshay Patil, and Steven S. Skiena. 2010. "Access: News and Blog Analysis for the Social Sciences." Paper presented to the nineteenth International World Wide Web Conference. Raleigh, N.C. (April 26–30).

Bernstein, Michael J., Steven G. Young, and Heather M. Claypool. 2010. "Is Obama's Win a Gain for Blacks? Changes in Implicit Racial Prejudice Following the 2008 Election." *Social Psychology* 41(3): 147–51.

Blanchard, Fletcher A., Christian S. Crandall, John C. Brigham, and Leigh Ann Vaughn. 1994. "Condemning and Condoning Racism: A Social Context Approach to Interracial Settings." *Journal of Applied Psychology* 79(6): 993–97.

Blanchard, Fletcher A., Teri Lilly, and Leigh Ann Vaughn. 1991. "Reducing the Expression of Racial Prejudice." *Psychological Science* 2(2): 101–5.

Blanton, Hart, and James Jaccard. 2008. "Unconscious Racism: A Concept in Pursuit of a Measure." *Annual Review of Sociology* 34: 277–97.

Bobo, Lawrence D., Camille Z. Charles, Maria Krysan, and Alicia D. Simmons. 2012. "The *Real* Record on Racial Attitudes." In *Social Trends in American Life: Findings from the General Social Survey Since 1972,* edited by Peter V. Marsden. Princeton, N.J.: Princeton University Press.

Bobo, Lawrence, and James R. Kluegel. 1993. "Opposition to Race-Targeting: Self-Interest, Stratification Ideology, or Racial Attitudes?" *American Sociological Review* 58(4): 443–64.

———. 1997. "Status, Ideology, and Dimensions of Whites' Racial Beliefs and Attitudes: Progress and Stagnation." In *Racial Attitudes in the 1990s: Continuity and Change,* edited by Steven A. Tuch and Jack K. Martin. Westport, Conn.: Praeger.

Bodenhausen, Galen V., Norbert Schwarz, Herbert Bless, and Michaela Wanke. 1995. "Effects of Atypical Exemplars on Racial Beliefs: Enlightened Racism or Generalized Appraisals?" *Journal of Experimental Social Psychology* 31: 48–63.

Brewer, Marilynn B. 1999. "The Psychology of Prejudice: Ingroup Love and Outgroup Hate?" *Journal of Social Issues* 55(3): 429–44.

Brewer, Marilynn B., Valerie Dull, and Layton Lui. 1981. "Perceptions of the Elderly: Stereotypes as Prototypes." *Journal of Personality and Social Psychology* 41(4): 656–70.

Brewer, Marilynn B., and Norman Miller. 1984. "Beyond the Contact Hypothesis: Theoretical Perspectives on Desegregation." In *Groups in Contact: The Psychology of Desegregation,* edited by Norman Miller and Marilynn B. Brewer. Orlando, Fla.: Academic Press.

Brody, Gene H., Yi-Fu Chen, Velma McBride Murry, Xiaojia Ge, Ronald L. Simons, Frederick X. Gibbons, Meg Gerrard, and Carolyn E. Cutrona. 2006. "Perceived Discrimination and the Adjustment of African American Youths: A Five-Year Longitudinal Analysis with Contextual Moderation Effects." *Child Development* 77(5): 1170–89.

Brown, Rupert, and Miles Hewstone. 2005. "An Integrative Theory of Intergroup Contact." *Advances in Experimental Social Psychology* 37: 255–343.

Carmines, Edward G., Paul M. Sniderman, and Beth C. Easter. 2011. "On the Meaning, Measurement, and Implications of Racial Resentment." *Annals of the American Academy of Political and Social Science* 634(1): 98–116.

Cassisi, Jeffrey, Dennis R. Combs, Chris Michael, and David L. Penn. 2006. "Perceived Racism as a Predictor of Paranoia Among African Americans." *Journal of Black Psychology* 32(1): 87–104.

Charles, Camille Z. 2003. "The Dynamics of Racial Segregation." *Annual Review of Sociology* 29: 167–207.

———. 2006. *Won't You Be My Neighbor? Race, Class, and Residence in Los Angeles.* New York: Russell Sage Foundation.

Coates, Ta-Nehisi. 2012. "Fear of a Black President." *The Atlantic* (September). Available at: http://www.theatlantic.com/magazine/archive/2012/09/fear-of-a-black-president/309064/ (accessed March 21, 2014).

Columb, Corey, and E. Ashby Plant. 2011. "Revisiting the Obama Effect: Exposure to Obama Reduces Implicit Prejudice." *Journal of Experimental Social Psychology* 47(2): 499–501.

Cooper, Eunice, and Marie Jahoda. 1947. "The Evasion of Propaganda: How Prejudiced People Respond to Anti-Prejudice Propaganda." *Journal of Psychology* 23(1): 15–25.

Dasgupta, Nilanjana, and Shaki Asgari. 2004. "Seeing Is Believing: Exposure to Counterstereotypic Women Leaders and Its Effect on the Malleability of Automatic Gender Stereotyping." *Journal of Experimental Social Psychology* 40(5): 642–58.

Dasgupta, Nilanjana, and Anthony G. Greenwald. 2001. "On the Malleability of Automatic Attitudes: Combating Automatic Prejudice with Images of Admired and Disliked Individuals." *Journal of Personality and Social Psychology* 81(5): 800–14.

Devine, Patricia G. 1989. "Stereotypes and Prejudice: Their Automatic and Controlled Components." *Journal of Personality and Social Psychology* 56(1): 5–18.

Dilliplane, Susanna. 2011. "All the News You Want to Hear: The Impact of Partisan News Exposure on Political Participation." *Public Opinion Quarterly* 75(2): 287–316.

Dilliplane, Susanna, Seth K. Goldman, and Diana C. Mutz. 2013. "Televised Exposure to Politics: New Measures for a Fragmented Media Environment." *American Journal of Political Science* 57(1): 236–48.

Dixon, Jeffrey C., and Michael S. Rosenbaum. 2004. "Nice to Know You? Testing Contact, Cultural, and Group Threat Theories of Anti-Black and Anti-Hispanic Stereotypes." *Social Science Quarterly* 85(2): 257–79.

Dixon, Travis L. 2008. "Network News and Racial Beliefs: Exploring the Connection Between National Television News Exposure and Stereotypical Perceptions of African Americans." *Journal of Communication* 58(2): 321–37.

Dovidio, John F., Samuel L. Gaertner, Ana Validzic, Kimberly Matoka, Brenda Johnson, and Stacy Frazier. 1997. "Extending the Benefits of Recategorization: Evaluations, Self-disclosure, and Helping." *Journal of Experimental Social Psychology* 33(4): 401–20.

Druckman, James N., Jordan Fein, and Thomas J. Leeper. 2012. "A Source of Bias in Public Opinion Stability." *American Political Science Review* 106(2): 430–54.

England, Paula, Paul Allison, and Yuxiao Wu. 2007. "Does Bad Pay Cause Occupations to Feminize, Does Feminization Reduce Pay, and How Can We Tell with Longitudinal Data?" *Social Science* 36(3): 1237–56.

Ensari, Nurcan, and Norman Miller. 2002. "The Out-group Must Not Be So Bad After All: The Effects of Disclosure, Typicality, and Salience on Intergroup Bias." *Journal of Personality and Social Psychology* 83(2): 313–29.

Entman, Robert M., and Andrew Rojecki. 2000. *The Black Image in the White Mind: Media and Race in America.* Chicago: University of Chicago Press.

Fazio, Russell H., Joni R. Jackson, Bridget C. Dunton, and Carol J. Williams. 1995. "Variability in Automatic Activation as an Unobtrusive Measure of Racial Attitudes: A Bona Fide Pipeline?" *Journal of Personality and Social Psychology* 69(6): 1013–27.

Federico, Christopher M. 2004. "When Do Welfare Attitudes Become Racialized? The Paradoxical Effects of Education." *American Journal of Political Science* 48(2): 374–91.

Federico, Christopher M., and Jim Sidanius. 2002. "Sophistication and the Antecedents of Whites' Racial Policy Attitudes: Racism, Ideology, and Affirmative Action in America." *Public Opinion Quarterly* 66(2): 145–76.

Feldman, Stanley, and Leonie Huddy. 2005. "Racial Resentment and White Opposition to Race-Conscious Programs: Principles or Prejudice?" *American Journal of Political Science* 49(1): 168–83.

Fields, Barbara J., and Karen Fields. 2012. *Racecraft: The Soul of Inequality in American Life.* London: Verso.

Fiske, Susan T. 1980. "Attention and Weight in Person Perception: The Impact of Negative and Extreme Behavior." *Journal of Personality and Social Psychology* 38(6): 889–906.

Ford, Thomas E. 1997. "Effects of Stereotypical Television Portrayals of African-Americans on Person Perception." *Social Psychology Quarterly* 60(3): 266–75.

Gaertner, Samuel L., and John F. Dovidio. 2000. *Reducing Intergroup Bias: The Common Ingroup Identity Model.* Hove, U.K.: Psychology Press.

———. 2005. "Understanding and Addressing Contemporary Racism: From Aversive Racism to the Common Ingroup Identity Model." *Journal of Social Issues* 61(3): 615–39.

Gaertner, Samuel L., John F. Dovidio, and Betty A. Bachman. 1996. "Revisiting the Contact Hypothesis: The Induction of a Common Ingroup Identity." *International Journal of Intercultural Relations* 20(3–4): 271–90.

Gaertner, Samuel L., Jeffrey Mann, John F. Dovidio, Audrey J. Murrell, and Marina Pomare. 1990. "How Does Cooperation Reduce Intergroup Bias?" *Journal of Personality and Social Psychology* 59(4): 692–704.

Gaertner, Samuel L., Jeffrey Mann, Audrey Murrell, and John F. Dovidio. 1989. "Reducing Intergroup Bias: The Benefits of Recategorization." *Journal of Personality and Social Psychology* 57(2): 239–49.

Gaertner, Samuel L., Mary C. Rust, John F. Dovidio, Betty A. Bachman, and Phyllis A. Anastasio. 1994. "The Contact Hypothesis: The Role of a Common Ingroup Identity in Reducing Intergroup Bias." *Small Group Research* 25(2): 224–49.

Gilens, Martin. 2000. *Why Americans Hate Welfare: Race, Media, and the Politics of Antipoverty Policy.* Chicago: University of Chicago Press.

Glaser, James N., and Timothy J. Ryan. 2013. *Changing Minds, If Not Hearts: Political Remedies for Racial Conflict.* Philadelphia: University of Pennsylvania Press.

Goldman, Seth K. 2012. "Effects of the 2008 Obama Presidential Campaign on White Racial Prejudice." *Public Opinion Quarterly* 76(4): 663–87.

Goldman, Seth K., Diana C. Mutz, and Susanna Dilliplane. 2013. "All Virtue Is Relative: A Response to Prior." *Political Communication* 30(4): 635–53.

González, Roberto, and Rupert Brown. 2003. "Generalization of Positive Attitude as a Function of Subgroup and Superordinate Group Identifications in Intergroup Contact." *European Journal of Social Psychology* 33(2): 195–214.

Grabe, Maria E., Matthew Lombard, Robert D. Reich, Cheryl C. Bracken, and Theresa B. Ditton. 1999. "The Role of Screen Size in Viewer Experiences of Media Content." *Visual Communication Quarterly* 6(2): 4–9.

Green, Donald P., and Rachel L. Seher. 2003. "What Role Does Prejudice Play in Ethnic Conflict?" *Annual Review of Political Science* 6: 509–31.

Greenwald, Anthony G., and Mahzarin R. Banaji. 1995. "Implicit Social Cognition: Attitudes, Self-esteem, and Stereotypes." *Psychological Review* 102(1): 4–27.

Greenwald, Anthony G., Debbie E. McGhee, and Jordan L. K. Schwartz. 1998. "Measuring Individual Differences in Implicit Cognition: The Implicit Association Test." *Journal of Personality and Social Psychology* 74(6): 1464–80.

Greenwald, Anthony G., Colin Tucker Smith, N. Sriram, Yoav Bar-Anan, and Brian A. Nosek. 2009. "Implicit Race Attitudes Predicted Vote in the 2008 U.S. Presidential Election." *Analyses of Social Issues and Public Policy* 9(1): 241–53.

Gross, Larry. 1984. "The Cultivation of Intolerance: Television, Blacks, and Gays." In *Cultural Indicators: An International Symposium,* edited by Gabriele Melischek, Karl E. Rosengren, and James Stappers. Vienna: Osterreichische Akademie der Wissenschaften.

Gurwitz, Sharon B., and Kenneth A. Dodge. 1977. "Effects of Confirmations and Disconfirmations on Stereotype-Based Attributions." *Journal of Personality and Social Psychology* 35(7): 495–500.

Hajnal, Zoltan H. 2001. "White Residents, Black Incumbents, and a Declining Racial Divide." *American Political Science Review* 95: 603–17.

———. 2007. *Changing White Attitudes Toward Black Political Leadership.* Cambridge: Cambridge University Press.

Halaby, Charles N. 2004. "Panel Models in Sociological Research: Theory into Practice." *Annual Review of Sociology* 30: 507–44.

Hamilton, David L. 1981. *Cognitive Processes in Stereotyping and Intergroup Behaviors.* Hillsdale, N.J.: Lawrence Erlbaum Associates.

Heise, David R. 1969. "Separating Reliability and Stability in Test–Retest Correlation." *American Sociological Review* 34(1): 93–101.

Henry, P. J., and David O. Sears. 2002. "The Symbolic Racism 2000 Scale." *Political Psychology* 23(2): 253–83.

Hollinger, David A. 2011. "The Concept of Post-Racial: How Its Easy Dismissal Obscures Important Questions." *Daedalus* 140(1): 174–82.

Huber, Gregory A., and Kevin Arceneaux. 2007. "Identifying the Persuasive Effects of Presidential Advertising." *American Journal of Political Science* 51(4): 961–81.

Huddy, Leonie, and Stanley Feldman. 2009. "On Assessing the Political Effects of Racial Prejudice." *Annual Review of Political Science* 12: 423–47.

Hurtwitz, John, and Mark Peffley. 1997. "Public Perceptions of Race and Crime: The Role of Racial Stereotypes." *American Journal of Political Science* 41(April): 375–401.

———. 2005. "Playing the Race Card in the Post-Willie Horton Era: The Impact of Racialized Code Words on Support for Punitive Crime Policy." *Public Opinion Quarterly* 69(1): 99–112.

Hutchings, Vincent L. 2009. "Change or More of the Same? Evaluating Racial Attitudes in the Obama Era." *Public Opinion Quarterly* 73(5): 917–42.

Jackman, Mary R. 1978. "General and Applied Tolerance: Does Education Increase Commitment to Racial Integration?" *American Journal of Political Science* 22(2): 302–24.

———. 1981. "Education and Policy Commitment to Racial Integration." *American Journal of Political Science* 25(2): 256–69.

———. 1994. *The Velvet Glove: Paternalism and Conflict in Gender, Class, and Race.* Berkeley: University of California Press.

Jackman, Mary R., and Michael J. Muha. 1984. "Education and Intergroup Attitudes: Moral Enlightenment, Superficial Democratic Commitment, or Ideological Refinement?" *American Sociological Review* 49(6): 751–69.

Jackson, John L., Jr. 2008a. *Racial Paranoia: The Unintended Consequences of Political Correctness.* New York: Basic Civitas.

———. 2008b. "Racial Paranoia vs. Bluffing About Race." *Chronicle of Higher Education,* July 17, 2008.

James, Sherman A., David S. Strogatz, Steve B. Wing, and Diane L. Ramsey. 1987. "Socioeconomic Status, John Henryism, and Hypertension in Blacks and Whites." *American Journal of Epidemiology* 126(4): 664–73.

Jhally, Sut, and Justin M. Lewis. 1992. *Enlightened Racism: The Cosby Show, Audiences, and the Myth of the American Dream.* Boulder, Colo.: Westview Press.

Kaiser, Cheryl R., Benjamin J. Drury, Kerry E. Spalding, Sapna Cheryan, and Laurie T. O'Brien. 2009. "The Ironic Consequences of Obama's Election: Decreased Support for Social Justice." *Journal of Experimental Social Psychology* 45(3): 556–59.

Kalmoe, Nathan A., and Spencer Piston. 2013. "Is Implicit Prejudice Against Blacks Politically Consequential? Evidence from the AMP." *Public Opinion Quarterly* 77(1): 305–22.

Kam, Cindy D., and Donald R. Kinder. 2007. "Terror and Ethnocentrism: Foundations of American Support for the War on Terrorism." *Journal of Politics* 69(2): 320–38.

———. 2012. "Ethnocentrism as a Short-Term Force in the 2008 Presidential Election." *American Journal of Political Science* 56(2): 326–40.

Katz, Elihu, and Paul F. Lazarsfeld. 1955. *Personal Influence: The Part Played by People in the Flow of Mass Communications.* New York: Free Press.

Kendall, P. L., and K. M. Wolf. 1949. "The Analysis of Deviant Case Studies in Communications Research." In *Communications Research 1948–1949,* edited by Paul F. Lazarsfeld and Frank N. Stanton. New York: Harper.

Kenski, Kate, Bruce W. Hardy, and Kathleen Hall Jamieson. 2010. *The Obama Victory: How Media, Money, and Message Shaped the 2008 Election.* Oxford: Oxford University Press.

Key, Ellen, Leonie Huddy, Matthew Lebo, and Steven S. Skiena. 2010. "Large-Scale Online Text Analysis Using Lydia." Paper presented to the annual meeting of the American Political Science Association. Washington, D.C. (September 1–5).

Kinder, Donald R., and Allison Dale-Riddle. 2012. *The End of Race? Obama, 2008, and Racial Politics in America.* New Haven, Conn.: Yale University Press.

Kinder, Donald R., and Katherine W. Drake. 2009. "Myrdal's Prediction." *Political Psychology* 30(4): 539–68.

Kinder, Donald R., and Cindy D. Kam. 2009. *Us Against Them: Ethnocentric Foundations of American Opinion.* Chicago: University of Chicago Press.

Kinder, Donald R., and Corrine M. McConnaughy. 2006. "Military Triumph, Racial Transcendence, and Colin Powell." *Public Opinion Quarterly* 70(2): 139–65.

Kinder, Donald R., and Tali Mendelberg. 1995. "Cracks in American Apartheid: The Political Impact of Prejudice Among Desegregated Whites." *Journal of Politics* 57: 402–24.

———. 2000. "Individualism Reconsidered: Principles and Prejudice in Contemporary American Opinion." In *Racialized Politics: The Debate About Racism in America,* edited by David O. Sears, James Sidanius, and Lawrence Bobo. Chicago: University of Chicago Press.

Kinder, Donald R., and Lynn M. Sanders. 1996. *Divided by Color: Racial Politics and Democratic Ideals.* Chicago: University of Chicago Press.

Kinder, Donald R., and David O. Sears. 1981. "Prejudice and Politics: Symbolic Racism Versus Racial Threats to the Good Life." *Journal of Personality and Social Psychology* 40(3): 414–31.

Krysan, Maria. 1998. "Privacy and the Expression of White Racial Attitudes." *Public Opinion Quarterly* 62(4): 506–44.

Kuklinski, James H., and Michael D. Cobb. 1998. "When White Southerners Converse About Race." In *Perception and Prejudice: Race and Politics in the United*

States, edited by Jon Hurwitz and Mark Peffley. New Haven, Conn.: Yale University Press.

Kuklinski, James H., Michael D. Cobb, and Martin Gilens. 1997. "Racial Attitudes and the 'New South.'" *Journal of Politics* 59(2): 323–49.

Lee, Barrett A., Chad R. Farrell, and Bruce G. Link. 2004. "Revisiting the Contact Hypothesis: The Case of Public Exposure to Homelessness." *American Sociological Review* 69(1): 40–63.

Lloyd, Levon, Dimitrios Kechagias, and Steven S. Skiena. 2005. "Lydia: A System for Large-Scale News Analysis." *12th Symposium of String Processing and Information Retrieval: Lecture Notes in Computer Science* 3772: 161–66.

Logan, John. 2001. "Ethnic Diversity Grows, Neighborhood Integration Lags Behind." Report by the Lewis Mumford Center. University at Albany, State University of New York.

Lombard, Matthew, Robert D. Reich, Maria E. Grabe, Cheryl C. Bracken, and Theresa B. Ditton. 2000. "Presence and Television: The Role of Screen Size." *Human Communication Research* 26(1): 75–98.

Lowery, Brian S., Curtis D. Hardin, and Stacey Sinclair. 2001. "Social Influence Effects on Racial Prejudice." *Journal of Personality and Social Psychology* 81(5): 842–55.

Macrae, C. Neil, Galen V. Bodenhausen, and Alan B. Milne. 1998. "Saying No to Unwanted Thoughts: Self-focus and the Regulation of Mental Life." *Journal of Personality and Social Psychology* 74(3): 578–89.

Macrae, C. Neil, Galen V. Bodenhausen, Alan B. Milne, and Jolanda Jetten. 1994. "Out of Mind but Back in Sight: Stereotypes on the Rebound." *Journal of Personality and Social Psychology* 67(5): 808–17.

Macrae, C. Neil, Miles Hewstone, and Riana G. Griffith. 1993. "Processing Load and Memory for Stereotype-Based Information." *European Journal of Social Psychology* 23(1): 77–87.

Maoz, Ifat. 2003. "Peace-Building with the Hawks: Attitude Change of Jewish-Israeli Hawks and Doves Following Dialogue Encounters with Palestinians." *International Journal of Intercultural Relations* 27(6): 701–14.

Marx, David M., Sei Jin Ko, and Ray A. Friedman. 2009. "The 'Obama Effect': How a Salient Role Model Reduces Race-Based Performance Differences." *Journal of Experimental Social Psychology* 45(4): 953–56.

McCauley, Clark, Christopher L. Stitt, and Mary Segal. 1980. "Stereotyping: From Prejudice to Prediction." *Psychological Bulletin* 80(1): 195–208.

Mendelberg, Tali. 2001. *The Race Card: Campaign Strategy, Implicit Messages, and the Norm of Equality.* Princeton, N.J.: Princeton University Press.

Miller, Norman. 2002. "Personalization and the Promise of Contact Theory." *Journal of Social Issues* 58(2): 387–410.

Mitchell, Jason P., Brian A. Nosek, and Mahzarin R. Banaji. 2003. "Contextual Variations in Implicit Evaluation." *Journal of Experimental Social Psychology* 132(3): 455–69.

Monteith, Margo J., Leslie Ashburn-Nardo, Corrine I. Voils, and Alexander M. Czopp. 2002. "Putting the Brakes on Prejudice: On the Development and Operation of Cues for Control." *Journal of Personality and Social Psychology* 83(5): 1029–50.

Monteith, Margo J., Nicole E. Deneen, and Gregory D. Tooman. 1996. "The Effect of Social Norm Activation on the Expression of Opinions Concerning Gay Men and Blacks." *Basic and Applied Social Psychology* 18(3): 267–88.

Monteith, Margo J., Jeffrey W. Sherman, and Patricia G. Devine. 1998. "Suppression as a Stereotype Control Strategy." *Personality and Social Psychology Review* 2(1): 63–82.

Monteith, Margo J., Clarence V. Spicer, and Gregory D. Tooman. 1998. "Consequences of Stereotype Suppression: Stereotypes on AND Not on the Rebound." *Journal of Experimental Social Psychology* 34(4): 355–77.

Morgan, Michael. 1982. "Television and Adolescents' Sex Role Stereotypes: A Longitudinal Study." *Journal of Personality and Social Psychology* 43(5): 947–55.

———. 1987. "Television, Sex-Role Attitudes, and Sex-Role Behavior." *Journal of Early Adolescence* 7(3): 269–82.

Mutz, Diana C., and Seth K. Goldman. 2010. "Mass Media." In *The Sage Handbook of Prejudice, Stereotyping, and Discrimination,* edited by John F. Dovidio, Miles Hewstone, Peter Glick, and Victoria M. Esses. Thousand Oaks, Calif.: Sage Publications.

Nier, Jason A., Samuel L. Gaertner, John F. Dovidio, Brender S. Banker, Christine M. Ward, and Mary C. Rust. 2001. "Changing Interracial Evaluations and Behavior: The Effects of a Common Group Identity." *Group Processes and Intergroup Relations* 4(4): 299–316.

Olson, Michael A., and Russell H. Fazio. 2004. "Reducing the Influence of Extrapersonal Associations on the Implicit Association Test: Personalizing the IAT." *Journal of Personality and Social Psychology* 86(5): 653–67.

Oppliger, Patricia A. 2007. "Effects of Gender Stereotyping on Socialization." In *Mass Media Effects Research: Advances through Meta-Analysis,* edited by Raymond W. Preiss, Barbara Mae Gayle, Nancy Burrell, and Mike Allen. Mahwah, N.J.: Lawrence Erlbaum Associates.

Page-Gould, Elizabeth, Rodolfo Mendoza-Denton, and Linda R. Tropp. 2008. "With a Little Help from My Cross-Group Friend: Reducing Anxiety in Intergroup Contexts Through Cross-Group Friendship." *Journal of Personality and Social Psychology* 95(5): 1080–94.

Paluck, Elizabeth L. 2009. "Reducing Intergroup Prejudice and Conflict Using the Media: A Field Experiment in Rwanda." *Journal of Personality and Social Psychology* 96(3): 574–87.

Paluck, Elizabeth L., and Donald P. Green. 2009. "Prejudice Reduction: What Works? A Review and Assessment of Research and Practice." *Annual Review of Psychology* 60: 339–67.

Paolini, Stefania, Miles Hewstone, Ed Cairns, and Alberto Voci. 2004. "Effects of Direct and Indirect Cross-Group Friendships on Judgments of Catholics and Protestants in Northern Ireland: The Mediating Role of an Anxiety-Reducing Mechanism." *Personality and Social Psychology Bulletin* 30(6): 770–86.

Paradies, Yin. 2006. "A Systematic Review of Empirical Research on Self-reported Racism and Health." *International Journal of Epidemiology* 35(4): 888–901.

Pasek, Josh, Alexander Tahk, Yphtach Lelkes, Jon A. Krosnick, B. Keith Payne, Omair Akhtar, and Trevor Tompson. 2009. "Determinants of Turnout and Candidate Choice in the 2008 U.S. Presidential Election: Illuminating the Impact of Racial Prejudice and Other Considerations." *Public Opinion Quarterly* 73(5): 943–94.

Payne, B. Keith, Clara Michelle Cheng, Olesya Govorun, and Brandon D. Stewart. 2005. "An Inkblot for Attitudes: Affect Misattribution as Implicit Measurement." *Journal of Personality and Social Psychology* 89(3): 277–93.

Payne, B. Keith, Jon A. Krosnick, Josh Pasek, Yphtach Lelkes, Omair Akhtar, and Trevor Tompson. 2010. "Implicit and Explicit Prejudice in the 2008 American Presidential Election." *Journal of Experimental Social Psychology* 46(2): 367–74.

Peffley, Mark, Jon Hurwitz, and Paul M. Sniderman. 1997. "Racial Stereotypes and Whites' Political Views of Blacks in the Context of Welfare and Crime." *American Journal of Political Science* 41(1): 30–60.

Pettigrew, Thomas F. 1998. "Intergroup Contact Theory." *Annual Review of Psychology* 49: 65–85.

Pettigrew, Thomas F., and Linda R. Tropp. 2006. "A Meta-Analytic Test of Intergroup Contact Theory." *Journal of Personality and Social Psychology* 90(5): 751–83.

———. 2011. *When Groups Meet: The Dynamics of Intergroup Contact.* New York: Psychology Press.

Pew Research Center. 2010. "Media, Race, and Obama's First Year: A Study of African Americans in U.S. News Coverage." Washington, D.C.: Pew Research Center Project for Excellence in Journalism.

Pieterse, Alex L., Nathan R. Todd, Helen A. Neville, and Robert T. Carter. 2012. "Perceived Racism and Mental Health Among Black American Adults: A Meta-Analytic Review." *Journal of Counseling Psychology* 59(1): 1–9.

Piston, Spencer. 2010. "How Explicit Racial Prejudice Hurt Obama in the 2008 Election." *Political Behavior* 32(4): 431–51.

Plant, E. Ashby, and Patricia G. Devine. 2003. "The Antecedents and Implications of Interracial Anxiety." *Personality and Social Psychology Bulletin* 29(6): 790–801.

Plant, E. Ashby, Patricia G. Devine, William T. L. Cox, Corey Columb, Saul L. Miller, Joanna Goplen, and B. Michelle Peruche. 2009. "The Obama Effect: Decreasing Implicit Prejudice and Stereotyping." *Journal of Experimental Social Psychology* 45(4): 961–64.

Power, J. Gerard, Sheila T. Murphy, and Gail Coover. 1996. "Priming Prejudice: How Stereotypes and Counter-Stereotypes Influence Attribution of Responsibility and Credibility Among Ingroups and Outgroups." *Human Communication Research* 23(1): 36–58.

Rabinowitz, Joshua L., David O. Sears, James Sidanius, and Jon A. Krosnick. 2009. "Why Do White Americans Oppose Race-Targeted Policies? Clarifying the Impact of Symbolic Racism." *Political Psychology* 30(5): 805–28.

Ramasubramanian, Srividya. 2011. "The Impact of Stereotypical Versus Counter-stereotypical Media Exemplars on Racial Attitudes, Causal Attributions, and Support for Affirmative Action." *Communication Research* 38(4): 497–516.

Reeves, Byron, Annie Lang, Eun Young Kim, and Deborah Tatar. 1999. "The Effects of Screen Size and Message Content on Attention and Arousal." *Media Psychology* 1(1): 49–67.

Reeves, Byron, and Clifford Nass. 1996. *The Media Equation: How People Treat Computers, Television, and New Media Like Real People and Places.* Stanford, Calif.: CSLI Publications.

Remnick, David. 2010. *The Bridge: The Life and Rise of Barack Obama.* New York: Alfred A. Knopf.

Richardson, John D. 2005. "Switching Social Identities: The Influence of Editorial Framing on Reader Attitudes Toward Affirmative Action and African Americans." *Communication Research* 32(4): 503–28.

Rossler, Patrick, and Hans-Bernd Brosius. 2001. "Do Talk Shows Cultivate Adolescents' Views of the World? A Prolonged-Exposure Experiment." *Journal of Communication* 51(1): 143–63.

Rothbart, Myron, and Oliver P. John. 1985. "Social Categorization and Behavioral Episodes: A Cognitive Analysis of the Effects of Intergroup Contact." *Journal of Social Issues* 41(3): 81–104.

Schiappa, Edward, Peter B. Gregg, and Dean E. Hewes. 2005. "The Parasocial Contact Hypothesis." *Communication Monographs* 72(1): 92–115.

Schmidt, Kathleen, and Brian A. Nosek. 2010. "Implicit (and Explicit) Racial Attitudes Barely Changed During Barack Obama's Presidential Campaign and Early Presidency." *Journal of Experimental Social Psychology* 46(2): 308–14.

Schuman, Howard, Charlotte Steeh, Lawrence Bobo, and Maria Krysan. 1997. *Racial Attitudes in America: Trends and Interpretations.* Cambridge, Mass.: Harvard University Press.

Schwarz, Norbert, and Herbert Bless. 1992a. "Constructing Reality and Its Alternatives: An Inclusion/Exclusion Model of Assimilation and Contrast Effects in Social Judgment." In *The Construction of Social Judgments,* edited by Leonard L. Martin and Abraham Tesser. Hillsdale, N.J.: Lawrence Erlbaum Associates.

———. 1992b. "Scandals and the Public's Trust in Politicians: Assimilation and Contrast Effects." *Personality and Social Psychology Bulletin* 18(5): 574–79.

Sears, David O., and Donald R. Kinder 1985. "Whites' Opposition to Busing: On Conceptualizing and Operationalizing Group Conflict." *Journal of Personality and Social Psychology* 48(5): 1141–47.

Signorielli, Nancy. 1989. "Television and Conceptions About Sex Roles: Maintaining Conventionality and the Status Quo." *Sex Roles* 21(5–6): 341–60.

Skowronski, John J., and Donal E. Carlston. 1987. "Social Judgment and Social Memory: The Role of Cue Diagnosticity in Negativity, Positivity, and Extremity Biases." *Journal of Personality and Social Psychology* 52(4): 689–99.

———. 1989. "Negativity and Extremity Biases in Impression Formation: A Review of Explanations." *Psychological Bulletin* 105(1): 131–42.

Smith, Eliot R., and Michael A. Zarate. 1992. "Exemplar-Based Model of Social Judgment." *Psychological Review* 99(1): 3–21.

Smith, Tom W. 2002. "Measuring Inter-Racial Friendships." *Social Science Research* 31(4): 576–93.

Sniderman, Paul M., Louk Hagendoorn, and Markus Prior. 2004. "Predisposing Factors and Situational Triggers: Exclusionary Reactions to Immigrant Minorities." *American Political Science Review* 98(1): 35–50.

Sniderman, Paul M., Thomas Piazza, Philip E. Tetlock, and Ann Kendrick. 1991. "The New Racism." *American Journal of Political Science* 35(2): 423–47.

Sniderman, Paul M., and Edward H. Stiglitz. 2008. "Race and the Moral Character of the Modern American Experience." *The Forum: A Journal of Applied Research in Contemporary Politics* 6(4): 1–15.

Steele, Claude M. 2010. *Whistling Vivaldi: How Stereotypes Affect Us and What We Can Do.* New York: W. W. Norton and Co.

Stephan, Walter G., and Cookie W. Stephan. 1985. "Intergroup Anxiety." *Journal of Social Issues* 41(3): 157–75.

Stryker, Jo Ellen, Ricardo J. Wray, Robert C. Hornik, and Itzik Yanovitzky. 2006. "Validation of Database Search Terms for Content Analysis: The Case of Cancer New Coverage." *Journalism and Communication Quarterly* 83(2): 413–30.

Tarman, Christopher, and David O. Sears. 2005. "The Conceptualization and Measurement of Symbolic Racism." *Journal of Politics* 67(3): 731–61.

Tesler, Michael, and David O. Sears. 2010. *Obama's Race: The 2008 Election and the Dream of a Post-Racial America.* Chicago: University of Chicago Press.

Transue, John E. 2007. "Identity Salience, Identity Acceptance, and Racial Policy Attitudes: American National Identity as a Uniting Force." *American Journal of Political Science* 51(1): 78–91.

Tuch, Steven A., and Michael Hughes. 1996. "Whites' Opposition to Race-Targeted Policies: One Cause or Many?" *Social Science Quarterly* 77(4): 778–88.

Turner, Rhiannon N., Richard J. Crisp, and Emily Lambert. 2007. "Imagining Intergroup Contact Can Improve Intergroup Attitudes." *Group Processes and Intergroup Relations* 10(4): 427–41.

Valentino, Nicholas A., and Ted Brader. 2011. "The Sword's Other Edge: Perceptions of Discrimination and Racial Policy Opinion After Obama." *Public Opinion Quarterly* 75(2): 201–26.

Vidmar, Neil, and Milton Rokeach. 1974. "Archie Bunker's Bigotry: A Study in Selective Perception and Exposure." *Journal of Communication* 24(1): 36–47.

Weber, Renee, and Jennifer Crocker. 1983. "Cognitive Processes in the Revision of Stereotypic Beliefs." *Journal of Personality and Social Psychology* 45(5): 961–77.

Welch, Susan, and Lee Sigelman. 2011. "The 'Obama Effect' and White Racial Attitudes." *Annals of the American Academy of Political and Social Science* 634(1): 207–20.

Williams, Bruce A., and Michael X. Delli Carpini. 2011. *After Broadcast News: Media Regimes, Democracy, and the New Information Environment.* Cambridge: Cambridge University Press.

Williams, David R., and Selina A. Mohammed. 2009. "Discrimination and Racial Disparities in Health: Evidence and Needed Research." *Journal of Behavioral Medicine* 32(1): 20–47.

Wilson, Thomas C. 2006. "Whites' Opposition to Affirmative Action: Rejection of Group-Based Preferences as Well as Rejection of Blacks." *Social Forces* 85(1): 111–20.

Wittenbrink, Bernd, Charles M. Judd, and Bernadette Park. 2001. "Spontaneous Prejudice in Context: Variability in Automatically Activated Attitudes." *Journal of Personality and Social Psychology* 81(5): 815–27.

Wright, Stephen C., Arthur Aron, Tracy McLaughlin-Volpe, and Stacy A. Ropp. 1997. "The Extended Contact Effect: Knowledge of Cross-Group Friendships and Prejudice." *Journal of Personality and Social Psychology* 73(1): 73–90.

Wyer, Natalie A., Jeffrey W. Sherman, and Steven J. Stroessner. 2000. "The Roles of Motivation and Ability in Controlling the Consequences of Stereotype Suppression." *Personality and Social Psychology Bulletin* 26(1): 13–25.

Zajonc, Robert B. 1968. "Attitudinal Effects of Mere Exposure." *Journal of Personality and Social Psychology* 9(2): 1–27.

Zaller, John R. 1996. "The Myth of Massive Media Impact Revived: New Support for a Discredited Idea." In *Political Persuasion and Attitude Change,* edited by Diana Mutz, Richard Brody, and Paul Sniderman. Ann Arbor: University of Michigan Press.

Zebrowitz, Leslie A., Benjamin White, and Kristin Wieneke. 2008. "Mere Exposure and Racial Prejudice: Exposure to Other-Race Faces Increases Liking for Strangers of That Race." *Social Cognition* 26(3): 259–75.

Zillmann, Dolf, and Hans-Bernd Brosius. 2000. *Exemplification in Communication: The Influence of Case Reports on the Perception of Issues.* Mahwah, N.J.: Lawrence Erlbaum Associates.

INDEX

Boldface numbers refer to figures and tables.